OVERTHINKING IS NOT THE SOLUTION

25 Ways to Reduce Stress, Eliminate Negative Thinking, Develop Mental Clarity and Master Your Emotions to Live on Purpose

D1715309

Robert J. Charles

CONTENTS

Your Free Gift

DOWNLOAD YOUR FREE BOOK, ENOUGH OVERTHINKING

Click the link below to receive it:

https://go.robertjcharles.com/EnoughOverthinking

Inside this book, you will discover:

- The physical effects of overthinking
- Its mental effects
- Its social effects

This book shows you 11 detailed ways that overthinking negatively affects your health on a daily basis.

In addition to getting "Enough Overthinking", you'll have an opportunity to get my new books for free.

Again, here is the link:

https://go.robertjcharles.com/EnoughOverthinking

You will also receive a **BONUS FREE 30 BIBLICAL PROMISES TO OVERCOME ANY CHALLENGE**, which are instrumental in solving your daily dilemmas.

DOWNLOAD YOUR FREE 30 BIBLICAL PROMISE TO OVERCOME ANY CHALLENGE

https://go.robertjcharles.com/30BiblicalPromises

Thee 30 Biblical Promises from God will give you strength and resilience to move forward

Here is the link:
https://go.robertjcharles.com/30BiblicalPromises

INTRODUCTION

Have you been feeling stressed lately? Do you struggle to quiet your racing thoughts? Do you feel lost in your own world, exhausted by constant worry? If so, you might be a chronic overthinker.

Overthinking can be described as excessive mental activity and worrying. It is essentially when your thoughts are running in circles and never letting you catch a break. You can overthink anything, from an upsetting memory to a pause in the conversation, and it often leads to anxiety—which can quickly have a negative impact on your wellbeing.

Today, overthinking is endemic to our global society. It is estimated that 60 million people in the United States alone suffer from anxiety. Although they come from different backgrounds and have varying personalities, almost all share one thing: overthinking. We live in demanding times that require a great deal of mental ability to function and succeed. Family responsibilities, financial constraints, mental trauma, relationship problems, and other issues may keep our minds working nearly 24 hours a day. Unfortunately, this state of constant stress frequently leads to anxiety, fear, and negative outcomes. At this point, too much thinking becomes a huge problem.

I can empathize with what you've been through. I understand the stressful predicament you've created for yourself, and how you've been sucked into the worry trap. But I also know that you're an empathic, driven individual who is struggling to navigate your life and to believe in yourself along the way. That's why I wrote this book, which is full of strategies to guide you through the difficulties and assist you in rewiring your brain, regaining control of your thoughts, and altering your mental patterns. Throughout this guide, I will present you with science-backed tips to get control of your emotions, achieve personal and professional fulfillment, and transform your life by putting an end to destructive thought patterns.

With the assistance of this book, you can not only overcome your repetitious, unhelpful negative thoughts, but also replace them with positive ones that bring peace, joy, and love into your life. This applies to how you approach everything, from small questions like "Should I buy these flowers?" to large ones such as "How am I going to spend the rest of my life?"

This book will show you how to shake off the burden of negative thoughts. You can reset your brain with unique mind training routines, allowing you to stop worrying and stressing all the time. Follow the simple exercises found in this book if you want to rewire your brain to stop overthinking and reduce stress and anxiety. This guide is the solution you've been seeking. Why not begin a new chapter in your life—one without space for tension, anxiety, or negativity? In this book you'll find new and healthier habits to declutter your mind and achieve inner balance.

While it's true that several books on the topic of overthinking have been written already, I want to point out why I believe writing another one was worthwhile and what this book provides that is unique. Overthinking is destroying lives around the world; in this book, I offer a fresh perspective on this problem: a spiritual perspective. I wanted to create a dependable, practical guide for disciples of Christ on how to conquer self-destructive thinking, avoid perfectionism, and rewire your brain. In researching useful techniques for overcoming stress and fostering positive habits, I left no stone unturned. When you reach the end of this game-changing book, you will recognize your own tendency to overthink and be able to take simple actions to rewire your brain, develop new, positive thought patterns, and stop undermining every decision you make by second-guessing yourself.

Our mind is simply incredible. No other word can better define it. It is capable of amazing things, both psychologically and physiologically. However, if we allow the constant upheaval of negative thoughts and anxiety to set up camp in our head, we'll end up with completely out-of-control, negative, disturbing thoughts that create feelings of helplessness, sorrow, confusion, and depression. Until you can learn how to control these thoughts and think effectively, you will never be at peace with yourself.

Effective thinking assists you in steering your life in the desired direction. A mind that overthinks is unproductive; it chases away opportunities for joy and peace that present themselves to you. Stop allowing your mind to entrap you. Reclaim control of your thoughts. The lessons contained in this book will take you from where you are now to where you want to be by not only teaching you how to make wise choices but also discussing why your current way of thinking is detrimental to your wellbeing and how positivity can significantly improve your outlook.

If you can relate to the feelings of anxiety and helplessness described above, and if you wish to change them, keep reading this book.

CHAPTER ONE

Overthinking

"Don't worry about anything; instead, pray about everything. Tell God what you need, and thank him for all he has done."

– Philippians 4:6 (NLT)

Lesson from Shakespeare: A beautiful flower may bloom from a very difficult situation

In April 1564, in Stratford-upon-Avon, north of London, England, Shakespeare was born. The single biggest worry of Shakespeare's time was public health and hygiene. Specifically, everyone was afraid of the bubonic plague—and they had good reason to be worried. The plague was a horrific and fatal infectious disease. The terrible outbreaks of the plague took the lives of vast numbers of individuals. In fact, millions upon millions of people in Europe ended up dying from the plague over the centuries.

At the time, no one fully understood the plague; medical authorities did not know exactly where the disease had originated, how it spread, or how to cure it. However, they did realize that a large sum of people crowded together increased the infection rate.

This situation took place throughout Shakespeare's lifetime. With strict quarantines and the help of the weather, the epidemic would slow, and social activities would resume their ordinary course; however, after a break of a few years, the disease would inevitably return and ravage the country once again. When the death rate reached a specific number in London, city authorities shut the theaters down, including the Globe, which was famous for producing Shakespeare's plays. They could not resume their activities until the death rates decreased.

Why have I recounted this story here? Well, Shakespeare lived his entire life under the dark cloud of the bubonic plague, but despite the gloomy outlook, he continued to follow his passion and worked hard to write and produce many plays. Not only did thousands gather to watch his plays in 16th century London, but his work went on to have a massive impact on the English language, on playwriting, and on culture as a whole. As a young boy,

Abraham Lincoln read Shakespeare to master English. Hundreds of words and phrases we use every day first appeared in his writings, and many people believe Shakespeare was the best English writer of all time.

Shakespeare took action and overcame his situation. No matter how depressing a situation can be, do not lose your focus and passion to the trap of overthinking. Even in difficult times, something remarkable may still arise. A beautiful flower may bloom from a very unexpected place. A masterpiece can come from chaotic circumstances. Do not despair in your difficult moments. Keep your faith in God. He will bring you through whatever obstacle you currently face.

Before we can fully understand this, we first need to learn what overthinking is and how it takes a toll on our life. Once you understand what's holding you back, you can start the journey of becoming victorious, joyful, and at peace.

What Is Overthinking?

What is overthinking? It can be anxiety about the past, fear of the present, or worries for the future. It is a cognitive process that involves excessive or obsessive thinking about something, whether it's an event, a decision, a conversation, or an idea. This usually results in even more stress for the overthinker, who feels there are too many possible outcomes if a situation does not work out correctly, leaving them feeling helpless. Overthinking generally causes us to spend too much time ruminating with no action taken to solve the problem, thus having either a neutral or a negative effect on our wellbeing.

When you overthink, one of two main outcomes can take place:

1. You become so immersed in ruminating on the problem at hand that you lose track of time. You struggle with insomnia for nights on end because you cannot shut off your mind when you lie down in bed. This negatively affects your mental and physical health.

2. You eventually realize that the solution to the problem was right in front of you all along; however, you lose interest in solving it because you've already made up your mind about the outcome and are convinced things will turn out badly, even though many other possibilities could occur.

These outcomes indicate how harmful overthinking can be and why you need to stop.

Overthinking leads to mental and physical stress. It also leads to frustration. Here's an example: let's say you're a brand-new business owner and you're getting ready to showcase your new brand to the public for the first time. You may feel anxious about what people are going to think of it compared to other products on the market. You may worry about whether they will like it at all, which leads you to worrying about failing in your business and having nothing to show for your hard work. You continue to overthink until you completely lose passion for debuting your brand because you've already decided how things are going to go down (badly) instead of taking a chance on the outcome. Unlike Shakespeare, you've allowed your circumstances to infiltrate your thoughts and take away your passion.

Does this sound like you?

Do you find yourself constantly asking, "Should I do this?", "Did I do the right thing?", or "How am I supposed to do that?" ... and then questioning your answer? Do you stay in this indecisive stage for extended periods of time? If so, it may indicate that you're overthinking. Here are a few other criteria you can use to determine whether or not you're an overthinker:

- a need for perfectionism
- constantly seeking the opinions of others
- insomnia
- burnout
- irritability
- hypochondria
- prolonged sadness
- a belief that you do not have control over your life

Since you're reading this book, let's assume you are, in fact, an overthinker. What can you do about it?

The answer to this is simple: thoughts are either conscious or unconscious, and you must take control of the conscious ones (to the best of your ability) in order to improve the unconscious ones. Unconscious thoughts just sort of bubble up without any interference on our part and usually center on negative events and feelings like worry, anxiety, or regret. In your conscious thoughts, however, you can work on making the best of your situation.

Causes and Symptoms

The next step is to evaluate and solve the problem of overthinking in your life. First, it is essential to know what makes you overthink. That can be challenging. Perhaps it's mental issues, such as depression and anxiety. Maybe your fear of embarrassment pushes you to overthink what you wear or how you act in front of other people. Other factors that can cause chronic overthinking include childhood abuse or neglect, trauma, perfectionism, or a genetic predisposition to overthinking. These factors can affect the quality of our decisions in different ways. We will discuss these causes in the following paragraphs.

Holding on to excessive worry

Research shows that severe anxiety is widespread among American teenagers (Garcia & O'Neil, 2021). Most of them are afraid of failing in their lives. They worry too much about the world around them, about their image in the eyes of others. It's no surprise that they worry about what others think about them, and this tendency often continues into adulthood.

The habit of constantly worrying that things could go wrong will push you to overthink. The negative images you develop in your mind will often feature the fear of failure. This drains your energy and your ability to make good decisions.

Instead of worrying about the future, understand that thinking positively and constructively about accomplishing your goals is more productive. Remember, the future is uncertain for everybody. No one knows what will happen tomorrow, and Christ told us not to worry about tomorrow (Matthew 6:34). Therefore, the best thing you can do about the future is pray, plan for it, and then let whatever happens happen.

Changing your mentality to focus more on your goals and achieving them will motivate you to live a life with a sense of direction. The best part is that the sense of optimism you develop will help you see all aspects of your life from a positive perspective, increasing your overall sense of happiness.

Negativity

Studies have shown that negativity is a common trait among those diagnosed with anxiety and depression (Kalin, 2020). Past research has found that people who have a higher occurrence of these types of negative thoughts experience more stress and anxiety, which leads to subconscious patterns of overthinking and concentration problems.

The problem isn't the level of stress or anxiety, but how often this kind of thought occurs and what you do about it. People who are prone to overthinking might want to prepare themselves for these negative thoughts and find coping mechanisms to keep their minds in check.

Headaches and dizziness

A headache is a sign that your mind and body need rest. If you pay attention to your thinking, you might notice that you're thinking about similar matters repeatedly. Dizziness, likewise, is a common symptom of the tension brought about by worry and might happen when you're stressed. Sometimes the dizziness can be so intense that it causes concentration, vision, and task performance problems. If you're experiencing headaches and dizziness on a regular basis, it's possible that you're over-analyzing things.

Of course, it's possible that these are symptoms of an underlying health problem, so it's wise to get these symptoms checked by a professional; however, if you are otherwise healthy, these symptoms might be a sign that you're worrying too much and having issues with anxiety.

Negative emotions

You can know whether you are overthinking by checking for the symptoms of depression. Subconscious negative thoughts can be a symptom of clinical depression. (Note that not everyone who has negative thoughts is clinically depressed, but it's something to watch out for.)

Other symptoms of depression include sadness, irritability, and an overall lack of interest in things that make you happy. You might also feel completely overwhelmed by the responsibilities your day-to-day life. It might feel easier to just stay in bed all day.

You could also have trouble concentrating and focusing on things around you. You might feel a lack of motivation to do anything but feel guilty for not doing anything, and even avoid social interactions with other people. If you are experiencing any of these symptoms, please seek help from a professional to get yourself feeling better.

Abstract thinking

This refers to thinking which goes beyond concrete realities. When you formulate theories to explain your observations, you engage in abstract thinking. This can be a useful skill, but it can also be detrimental if you're an overthinker. For example, when your business is not performing well, you might jump to the conclusion that it's because you're doing something wrong and begin ruminating over your shortcomings instead of considering other possibilities.

Avoidance

Avoidance means that you try to avoid doing something by using the decision-making process as an excuse; that is, you spend so much time going back and forth between options because you want to avoid having to choose anything at all.

Neglecting intuition

This occurs when you don't take into consideration the things you already know at the core of your being, and instead opt to overthink. Instead of following your gut instinct, you end up second-guessing your intuition and could make the wrong decisions.

Creating problems

You may also think in a way that creates problems that are not there. Certain situations are not as complex as you may perceive them to be. The problem at hand may only require a couple of minutes to solve, but when you overthink it, you make it much more complicated than it needs to be.

It is vital to focus on the bigger picture and not nitpick at the details. Try to see things as they are; don't complicate your life by thinking of potential problems.

Magnifying the issue

Usually, small problems require simple solutions. Unfortunately, sometimes we amplify these problems and develop overly complex ways to solve them. This is another form of overthinking. You're wasting your mental resources to come up with huge, elaborate solutions that don't match the scale of the problems you're experiencing.

Fear of failure

Fear of failure is not a new concept to most people. This motivates many of us to work hard. But for an overthinker, instead of letting that fear drive you to work towards a bright future, you let that fear grow inside you and consume your thoughts.

Fear of failing can be crippling. It can cause you to rethink your actions and motivations. It can prevent you from taking the initial step. It can cruelly eat away at your self-confidence if you allow it to, leaving you feeling utterly incapable of taking the necessary action to realize your goals.

A certain amount of dread can inspire you if you remain focused on the end objective. (For example, think of a public speaker who turns their nerves into excitement and motivation to give a fantastic speech.) Despite these nagging anxious thoughts, you can use the nervous energy to force yourself toward your goal.

Failure can be a helpful learning experience if we allow it to be. We all must fail occasionally to develop as individuals and improve.

Making irrelevant decisions

An overthinker may believe it is vital to make certain decisions that they are not actually required to make. For instance, you might be convinced that you need to plan out all of your major life decisions for the next several years right at this very moment, when in fact it is just fine to let life unfold before you and make decisions one at a time as they are presented to you.

Now that we've explored some of the symptoms and causes of overthinking, let's examine the three main forms of overthinking.

Three Forms of Overthinking

There are three dangerous forms of overthinking: ruminating, fear, and excessive worrying. Let's dive into each of these.

Ruminating—Rehashing the Past

Ruminating is obsessively going over a thought or problem repeatedly without ever coming to a conclusion. Whether it be repeating an old argument in your mind over and over or mentally replaying a mistake you made like a broken record, you just cannot seem to let the thought go no matter what. Ruminating is heavily connected with depression because this mental health condition causes you to remember the worst aspects of yourself continually.

You can see the self-defeating aspect of ruminating. It's one of the most dangerous things about overthinking because it paralyzes you and prevents you from taking action. What's the point if (according to your mind) you're just going to fail, no matter how hard you try, or it's already too late to turn things around from a previous bad decision? As you can see, rumination reflects how you view yourself and is thus deeply rooted in self-esteem and self-image.

If you've experienced any form of abuse, neglect, or trauma, it could result in lower self-esteem or self-image. This is further exacerbated if you have a history of academic, athletic, or social underperformance during your formative years and have been constantly compared to your higher-performing peers. Without any obvious talents to make you think otherwise, it's easy to feel like you're a nobody.

Fear for the Present

Fear for the present actually stems from the past. It is a reminder that things can be taken away in an instant and there is nothing you can do about it. If you find yourself constantly in a state of fear about what could happen to you or a loved one at any moment, you are experiencing this form of overthinking.

This feeling activates when you have something important on your mind and don't want anything else to stand in its way, whether it's a relationship or a work project. The fear hinders your productivity because you're constantly worrying about danger or failure. The anxiousness associated with this fear makes it difficult to concentrate on key tasks.

Another reason we may find it difficult to live in the present is that it is constantly filled with reminders of our mortality. Whether we realize it or not, we become acutely aware of life's relentless course. Change is the only constant.

However, if you relive the same scenario over and over again, whether it's about to happen or has already happened, you are being consumed by your thoughts. If you tend to get caught up in negative visions of the future, you are locked in "worry mode." We all do this to some degree, but the critical question is whether or not you have moved into addictive thinking territory. Just like an addiction to substances consumes a person with anxiety, worry, and doubt, being addicted to overthinking and overanalyzing creates a sense of being bound to suffering. It takes you over, and it isn't very easy to be present and in your body.

Why does this happen? Because underneath the fear, subtle or not, emotions are begging to be processed. For example, if you are nervous about an upcoming conversation, rather than being with and facing the fear, your brain will run every possible scenario to try to make you feel that you can control the outcome—to try to make you feel secure. This is not realistic. Don't be trapped by this false promise. The reality is, we can't control what happens in life and it's better to learn to live without the fear.

Excessive Worrying—Predicting the Future Negatively

Worry is your brain anticipating potential problems in order to avoid them, but this tends to lead to negative, usually disastrous future predictions:

- I'm going to fail the test tomorrow. I'll blank out, forget everything, and end up failing out of school.

- I'll never get my dream job. There's always going to be someone better than me. I should play it safe and work a stable and well-paying career I hate.

As you can see, ruminating and worrying are closely related; both cause one to think negatively, whether it be about oneself or a situation.

You may feel stressed about your presentation tomorrow, so you start to tell yourself that you won't do a good job. The more you think about it, the more you worry about what could go wrong, and the worse you feel. Or perhaps you have low self-esteem and feel that you aren't good enough, so you constantly worry that your spouse or partner will find someone else and leave you. Because you don't believe in yourself, you don't have confidence in how things will turn out; you are therefore always worrying about the future—fear of the unknown.

Rescuing Yourself from Overthinking

Overthinking is such a common cause of stress and anxiety that nearly everyone does it from time to time. At this point, you're probably wondering how you can put an end to all of this overthinking and the misery it can cause. Good news: the time for help is here. It's rescue time!

If you have identified yourself as an overthinker, here are some ideas for resolving the problem.

Be aware of the problem

Becoming aware of this problem is the first step to solving it. If you're not aware that your mind is wandering down negative paths towards anxiety and stress, how can you expect to stop it? Keeping track of your thoughts can help you see when you're getting stuck in a negative mental cycle, whether it's wondering what might happen if a specific event occurs or ruminating about what someone said to you yesterday.

Research shows that positive self-talk can positively impact your general wellbeing (Grzybowski, 2021). However, the impact of self-talk is only clear when you use it positively and consistently. The power of self-talk can lead to an overall boost in your self-esteem and confidence.

If you convince your inner-self that you are calm, confident, and capable of rising above any situation, you will find it easier to overcome the emotions that seem to weigh you down.

Prevent negative thoughts

Next, you can take preventative measures against your thoughts by preparing yourself for the worst. The best way to do this is to think through what would happen if the worst-case scenario were to occur. Run this scenario in your mind all the way through to the end.

For example, if you have a job performance review coming up and you're feeling extreme anxiety about it, follow your anxiety to its conclusion. What is the worst-case scenario? You might get a bad review. What's the worst thing that could happen if you got a bad review? You might be fired. Then what would you do? You could start polishing up your resume and applying for other jobs. If you play out the scenario like this, you might discover that even in the very worst case, you have the strength to overcome the situation. It might also be helpful to make a list of exactly what you'll do if you're left with limited options. Having a strategy for the worst-case scenario will put your mind at ease and help you see that there's always something that can be done, even in the scariest situations.

Talk to someone

Talking to someone about what's going on in your head can help calm your worries and ease your anxiety. If you have a trusted friend or family member you can confide in, this is one of the best ways to get your thoughts out in the open and find out exactly what's going through your head. Telling a friend about your feelings can help you see you aren't alone in your struggles and put things into perspective. It also allows your friend to offer advice and comfort. Finally, it will make you aware of how overthinking can affect your mental state so you'll be better prepared to prevent that negative spiral.

Take some time for yourself

It's essential to get some time for yourself each day or every week, even if it's just for 15 minutes. Do something that will make you feel more in control of your mind. Finding these coping mechanisms helps keep your thoughts and emotions in check when you're going through a rough time. If you're feeling spaced out, read a book, listen to music, or go for a walk. These things can help prop up your mood and relax your body.

Change your habits

Set a goal for what you want to accomplish each day or week, and try not to dedicate too much time to one thing. Keep your goals short and simple. For example, if your goal is to read each day, block out just 15 minutes a day for reading. If you make your goal too big and complex, you're less likely to follow through and this can lead to more stress and anxiety. Achieving small goals on a daily basis will help your concentration and improve your focus.

Take care of your health

Another important way to take control of your mind is to take care of your overall health. Get plenty of rest each night and exercise regularly. Try to get around eight hours of sleep every night. Of course, if you're already experiencing insomnia as a result of your overthinking, this might be easier said than done, but do what you can to make your bedroom a peaceful and relaxing place so that you can rest even if you're not asleep. These things are important for improving your mood and overall wellbeing.

Eating healthy food can also help keep you feeling balanced and in control of your emotions. If you're not taking care of yourself, you're not giving yourself the best chance to combat overthinking.

Talk to God

You can always talk to God about how you feel. He will always listen to your prayers and answer them because He knows what is best for you. Sometimes all it takes is a simple prayer to make things better again if you're feeling stressed out or worried.

God transforms believers. He will assist you with your mental confinement. As Luke chapter 4 tells us, Jesus is coming to liberate the captives. Jesus wants to deliver you from your mental jail. He has this power. He wants to help you in your battles. Remember that nothing is impossible with God. You can have your life back—you just need to trust Him.

The Apostle Paul wrote:

"Be anxious for nothing, but in everything by prayer and supplication, with thanksgiving, let your requests be made known to God; and the peace of God, which surpasses all

understanding, will guard your hearts and minds through Christ Jesus."

– Philippians 4:6-7 (NKJV)

Paul wrote these words as he was in jail, facing various horrible challenges that could have pushed him to overthink his situation and be filled with fear and anxiety. However, knowing that God is with him, he believes, and he dares to say to the Philippians, "Be anxious for nothing."

These two verses invite us to:

- Seek help from the Lord
- Praise God for His goodness
- Put your situations in God's hands
- Meditate and reflect on the good things around you.

Doing these things will give you peace. All of this is possible in Christ, and this attitude will help you overcome your tendency to overthink.

I want to remind you today, as Paul did the Philippians: "Be anxious for nothing."

Key Takeaways

- Overthinking can be anxiety about the past, fear of the present, or worries for the future. It is a cognitive process that involves excessive or obsessive thoughts about something, such as an event, decision, or idea.

- Rumination is a pattern of cyclical thinking over something that happened in the past. It is characterized by repeating the same thought without reaching a conclusion, usually accompanied by negative feelings and anxiety.

- Fear is a reaction to a present, perceived threat, and it impacts us both physically and emotionally. We find it difficult to live in the present if we are constantly filled with fear.

- Worrying about the future or about current events creates a stress response in the brain.

- Worrying itself is the process of expecting a negative outcome that may never occur. Once you've accepted the idea of something bad happening, it will constantly be in your mind.

- It's best to stop ruminating over negative thoughts, no matter how hard it is to let them go, because ruminating has detrimental effects on your life.

- The best thing you can do to rescue yourself from the negative thoughts is to pray and trust in God. He will help you through every situation.

Time to Take Action

I want you to realize you can do something right now to help you cope with overthinking. It's time to stop thinking about what occurred in the past or worrying about what will happen in the future and start living in the present.

This is the perfect time to take action. Don't let negative thoughts destroy your life. If you're ready to change your life for the better, then you can choose right now to live the best possible life you can.

If you're serious about taking your life back from those negative thoughts, you have to change. A new way of reasoning is required. It's best to start by taking some notes about what keeps your mind busy.

In the next chapter, we'll dive into the undesirable consequences of overthinking to demonstrate to gain a clear understanding of its effects on our mental and physical health as well as our relationships.

CHAPTER TWO

Undesirable Consequences of Overthinking

"A merry heart does good, like medicine, But a broken spirit dries the bones."

– Proverbs 17:22 (NKJV)

In case you're not already convinced of the serious impact that overthinking can have on your life, let's look at an example of how it can affect you over the course of your life.

Lia's overthinking journey

It all started when Lia was about 10 years old. It started with the small things, like picking a subject to start on for her homework or deciding which color pencil to use. Every time Lia had to make a choice, she spent lots of time considering which one would be best and what the outcomes might be.

In school, she was scared to disappoint her teachers, as her parents always told her school was her responsibility, and she was expected to have good grades. She was afraid of not being good enough, and she often prayed to be good. Because of all this stress and overthinking, Lia spent her childhood days feeling tired and lacking energy despite sleeping an adequate number of hours every night.

The tiredness turned into anxiety once Lia grew up and became a young lady. During her last years of high school, she had to choose a university, and during university she had to choose a career path, and every choice presented to her only added to her anxiety and doubts. She wanted everything to be perfect and wanted everyone around her to be happy. But, because of this, Lia spent way too much time thinking about her choices and about every little thing that could go wrong, over and over and over again.

By the time Lia started working her first job, her stomach had started to rebel. She frequently got really bad stomachaches, and eventually found out she had ulcers after a pretty severe case of stress and anxiety due to a problem she had at work. All Lia wanted was to be perfect, to please everyone, but in doing so, she spent too much time inside her head, worrying, and in turn, she had made her body sick too.

It took Lia a very long time to realize all her symptoms could be traced back to her overthinking. But once she did, she turned back to what she knew best: religion. She went to the Lord and asked Him for guidance, asked Him to help her to trust the process more and worry less about the outcome.

Lia had forgotten she was meant to trust, to believe. So, slowly, she worked on herself and tried to overthink less. The results didn't show up immediately, but Lia gradually found tips and tricks to help her live a better life, one free from overthinking.

Do you, like Lia, feel sick all the time? Have you lost sleep? Is your stomach constantly in knots? Have you had trouble finishing projects? If you've ruled out any physical causes of your symptoms, it's likely that you are overthinking and experiencing excessive stress and anxiety.

It was once thought that overthinking was merely an indication that one was worrying too much about what they were doing. Unfortunately, it has been found to have a lot more severe consequences than people originally thought. Overthinking hurts. Below is a list of the consequences that come with overthinking.

How Does Overthinking Affect Life?

Overthinking can be such a burden. Whether you're contemplating your next career move or thinking about your current relationship, it can be hard not to create an endless stream of worry and doubt. If you are indeed an overthinker, you overanalyze everything around you. You may try to find a deeper meaning in each of your experiences. When meeting new people, you may focus on how other people are perceiving you instead of engaging in productive communication. If someone gives you an unusual look, you may make assumptions about what they're thinking about you based on that glance.

Essentially, overthinking consumes you. You end up wasting a lot of energy trying to make sense of the world around you. What you don't recognize is that not everything has a deeper meaning. Sometimes a look from a colleague is just a casual look with no thought behind it, and sometimes people say things flippantly without having any deeper meaning.

As an overthinker, you've probably experienced something called "analysis paralysis." This is a scenario where you think so much about the outcomes of a decision and spend so much time weighing the options that you end up doing absolutely nothing—you're paralyzed by fear and anxiety. You may then find yourself in a vicious circle of thinking a lot, but doing very little. Perhaps the best strategy to prevent yourself from falling into this type of thinking trap is to try out each of the alternatives. The simple decision to act—no matter what that action is— will make a huge difference.

To understand why overthinking is one of the leading factors in anxiety and depression, you first need to know what's happening in your brain when you're worrying. When something bad arises or someone says something negative, our brains respond by releasing stress hormones like cortisol into the bloodstream. Cortisol speeds up the heart rate, raises blood pressure and tells the brain to release many other stress hormones. Overthinking can thus have many undesirable consequences on your life.

Can cause depression, ulcers, and colitis

Depression is a psychological condition that may manifest itself in various ways. It is a common, chronic illness. Estimates suggest that 1% of the global population is suffering from depression (Shah, Mohammad, Qureshi, Abbas, & Aleem, 2021).

To try to alleviate some of the worldwide burden of depression, the World Health Organization released a statement that defines depression as "a common mental disorder portrayed by persistent sadness or low mood that affects [one's] ability to function." A single factor or a combination of factors may bring depression about. Since every individual is unique, what motivates and depresses them differs.

The term "depression" is frequently portrayed as tragic, disheartening, sad, fractious, unmotivated. In general, it means the absence of intrigue or delight in life, which is often impacted by overthinking. When these feelings only exist for a brief timeframe, it might be a passing instance of "the blues." But if they continue over many days and begin to interfere with your ordinary daily life, chances are you might be clinically depressed.

Depression is more than a persistent state of bitterness. It is a psychological issue that requires professional care. Significant depression can manifest itself in a variety of ways; it can not only impact your emotions, but impact you physiologically as well. People with clinical depression are in danger of experiencing serious negative outcomes, especially individuals between 15 and 24 years old, as indicated by the American Psychological Association (APA) (Kalin, 2021).

People who are diagnosed with depression may struggle to eat, sleep, or do many other daily tasks. Having a significant amount of stress as a result increases the risk of heart disease, ulcers, and colitis, a chronic digestive disorder characterized by inflammation of the colon's inner lining.

Affects the heart

Symptoms of high stress levels often include an increased heart rate or a fast heartbeat. One study that examined the association between stress and rapid heartbeats discovered that a person's heart rate is much higher when going through a stressful situation (Low & McCraty, 2018).

When you can't stop your mind from ruminating and you're constantly thinking about stressful scenarios, the stress accumulates in your heart. While you're sitting there trying to think of all the things that could go wrong, your heart beats harder out of fear. As a result, the blood flow to your heart increases, causing an increase in pressure. This can eventually lead to a condition called hypertensive heart disease, when the arteries in one or both of your heart chambers become narrowed or blocked. As blood continues to travel through those blocked arteries, it can cause a heart attack.

You must realize that what we're talking about here is significant stress over prolonged periods of time. Naturally, a bit of stress and a racing heart here and there isn't going to cause any permanent harm. It's when you let the overthinking get out of control for weeks, months, and years that your health becomes jeopardized.

Increases cancer risk

When you keep thinking about negative issues and reinforcing a feeling of fear, your body can release chemicals that disrupt the normal balance of hormones.

The disruption of this balance increases your risk of developing cancer.

One of the most obvious victims of overthinking and stress is the brain—that's a no-brainer (forgive the pun). Stress has a significant impact on this organ. Cortisol (the stress hormone) can harm and even kill brain cells in the hippocampus. Chronic overthinking can change the structure and connectivity of the brain, altering its functions. Chronic stress also causes mental difficulties like anxiety and mood disorders (Andersson, Carlbring, Titov, & Lindefors, 2019).

Gets you stuck in analysis paralysis

We often cling to denial to prevent ourselves from having to endure the reality of stressful situations and uncomfortable or painful emotions. This manifests for many people in the form of addiction; they use distractions like drugs, alcohol, exercise, or work so that they don't have to face the truth. Unfortunately, this only exacerbates the problem because these shortcuts are not the solution. In a similar manner, some people become "addicted" to thinking, which leads to overthinking because they cannot or do not want to accept the truth.

Because of the aspiration for perfection, overthinkers continuously examine and re-examine any situation. They are afraid of making the wrong choice, and they're out of touch with their instincts. Therefore, they take a lot of time to make decisions, don't have confidence in their choices, and often end up not choosing anything at all—resulting in the previously discussed "analysis paralysis."

Social media and the internet only exacerbate the analysis paralysis an overthinker may experience by providing an unrealistic and idealized version of life. The result is a "perfect" standard that we feel obligated to meet to fit in, but of which we always fall short no matter what, resulting once again in endless anxiety, worry, and self-doubt. (If you want to see examples of this unrealistic standard, look no further than your Instagram feed.)

If you do not take control of the thoughts that are causing you to worry excessively, you'll end up with more stress, which (as discussed previously) is a leading cause of mental health problems. Providentially, this book will give you insights on how to stop worrying and therefore decrease the chance of any health problems arising so that you can live a healthier, happier life. If you make a "bad" decision, remind yourself that it's okay; it happens to everyone. The important thing is that you gained a lesson from your mistake.

Leads to anxiety

Anxiety is a physiological stress response that may be beneficial or harmful based on the level of the reaction. Everyone encounters anxiety from time to time; in fact, it is an imperative piece of our physiological makeup. It can encourage us to recognize and deal with difficult situations. Basically, anxiety allows us to distinguish and react to peril by entering "fight or flight" mode. The "ideal" amount of anxiety can actually assist us in performing better and overcoming challenges.

However, there is another side of anxiety. Certain people have intense and overwhelming anxiety responses that essentially hijack their brains and block them from rationally or reasonably processing their experiences.

Persistent anxiety causes genuine problems and can even lead to physical illness or anxiety disorders such as panic attacks, phobias, and obsessive-compulsive behaviors. Anxiety at this level can have a troubling and weakening effect on our lives and our physical and mental wellbeing, prompting a wide range of physical manifestations like headaches, digestive issues, and heart palpitations. The consequences of unchecked anxiety can be even more serious in the long haul, possibly causing permanent damage to our bodies.

Alarmingly, around 1 in 5 individuals report feeling anxious "almost constantly" or "much of the time." As a whole, it seems that we as a society perceive ourselves as being more anxious than in the past (Swift et al., 2014). A study by the Mental Health Foundation shows that money and responsibilities are two of the most common sources of anxiety. Anxiety is one of the most universally recognized mental medical issues globally, and it is essentially an epidemic in modern society; however, it is still under-studied, under-reported, and under-treated.

A decent capacity to adapt to anxiety is vital to withstanding whatever life tosses at us. Allowing extreme anxiety to build within us again and again increases our chances of being overcome by fear, unable to discover balance in our lives, or to relax and recoup.

Can kill relationships

You should grab the opportunity, whenever it's presented to you, to develop emotionally and personally with your spouse or partner. Only through this type of intimate partnership can you understand how to become more empathetic and present. Unfortunately, overthinking is one of the primary causes of conflict between partners, friends, and family members. While some people can talk out their issues, others avoid confronting their problems head-on, instead ruminating about them and growing cold or distant in the relationship.

This is a mistake. It's time for you to take responsibility for your actions and confront the source of your frustration. Most people overthink because they feel overwhelmed by the number of things in their lives that are out of their control.

Remember, there will never be a perfect relationship; your partner has flaws just as you do. Therefore, instead of turning to someone else to improve your relationships, a great place to begin is within yourself. Minimizing your own tension and anxiety will significantly boost your own quality of life and, by extension, the quality of your relationships.

Deciding to take back control of your thoughts is the start of a mindful partnership that will restore bonding instead of fostering conflict and disunity.

Signs of overthinking in a relationship

It's easy to drift through the day thinking about your significant other when you're in a relationship, especially if it's new and exciting. Thoughts about your coupledom are valid even as the relationship evolves and becomes more stable.

When those thoughts become increasingly negative or intrusive, however, and consume more and more of your time when you should be concentrating on other things, it's time to reign them in a little. When you obsess over minor details, over things expressed and things unsaid, what your partner did or did not do, your mind might fool you into thinking things that aren't true. These are symptoms of excessive thinking about a relationship:

- You continually imagine the worst-case scenario (for example, worrying about harm befalling your partner)

- You conjure up implausible scenarios in your head (such as unfaithfulness even though your partner has given you no reason to doubt him or her)

- You become illogical (for example, asking your partner to do things to "prove" his or her loyalty)

- You are unreasonably suspicious

- You have a rich imagination, but you use it to imagine negative situations

"What if" makes life miserable

It is astonishing to see the number of people who feel lonely these days. Even those with active social lives, who spend a lot of time with people, often develop a sense of loneliness. During the pandemic, these feelings of isolation have only increased throughout society. If a person does not have a supportive family, good friends, or even good neighbors, they can easily begin to feel lonely. Persistent feelings of isolation can lead to depression, and sometimes it also leads to excessive "What if?" thinking.

For example, you may begin to worry about things happening that have never happened before or imagine yourself in situations that have never occurred. You might catch yourself asking, "What if I say something wrong?", "What if it rains and I have to cancel my plans?", "What if so-and-so thinks such-and-such about me?", and so on. You're overthinking a situation before it even happens. And sadly, most of the time, your inner dialogue is negative. It's time to change that.

Avoiding taking action when you should

You may think the reason you're overthinking is because you want to make the best possible choice, but many times, you're actually avoiding taking action. When you're confronted with an issue that requires action, your first instinct is to overthink about what to do instead of simply doing something.

Think about the last few conversations you had that involved an issue you wanted to take action on or a problem you needed to solve. You probably thought about every aspect of the problem and came up with a list of reasons you couldn't solve it. This is essentially a form of procrastination. You're afraid of facing whatever the outcome might be, so you just avoid doing anything altogether.

Not accepting reality

Sometimes, people allow their emotions and bad memories to come into play when overthinking. When you have thoughts like "I'm terrible at handling challenges" or "I'm inadequate," this shows that your negative emotions are getting in the way. Accept the reality that you're not perfect and that sometimes people make mistakes, including you. Otherwise, your mind will create fear-based scenarios that will ultimately cause your emotions to control you instead of the other way around.

The Solution: Avoid Negativity

Doing anything negative, including overthinking, puts a barrier between you and the reality of the world around you. It also puts a barrier between you and God. When something negative happens, remind yourself that it's okay, and that life is not perfect. Overthinking only prolongs the bad feelings that are part of this reality. It's time to act instead of overthinking.

Think about the last time you overthought a problem. What was it? What did you tell yourself? How did it make you feel? Overthinking doesn't make any situation better, so don't think about any one issue for too long. Instead, set yourself a time limit to think over and confront the problem logically; then, take action on what you've learned or decided and don't look back.

Your thoughts need a curfew. Fill your mind with God's Living Word and you will have no space for the enemy's lies. God has many wonderful promises for you:

"Even to your old age, I am He, And even to gray hairs I will carry you! I have made, and I will bear; Even I will carry, and will deliver you."

– Isaiah 46:4 (NKJV)

"No weapon formed against you shall prosper, And every tongue which rises against you in judgment You shall condemn. This is the heritage of the servants of the Lord, And their righteousness is from Me, Says the Lord."

– Isaiah 54:17 (NKJV)

"Though the mountains be shaken and the hills be removed, yet my unfailing love for you will not be shaken nor my covenant of peace be removed, says the Lord, who has compassion on you."

– Isaiah 54:10 (NIV)

Key Takeaways

- Overthinking is often used as an easy way to avoid taking action.
- Overthinking can be caused by negative thoughts and emotions that distract you from reality.

- Not confronting issues is a form of overthinking, which prevents you from moving on with your life.

- Taking action on the problem at hand will allow you to move on with your life instead of thinking about it for too long.

- God has worked miracles for you in the past. He wants to do this for you again in the future, if you let Him.

Time to Take Action

Only when you take action can your mind turn positive thoughts into reality. The more you take action to solve your problems, the better life gets.

And, of course, the better you get at doing this, the more likely you are to be successful at it again. This is how habits are created. You can utilize the power of habits negatively (by letting yourself overthink and become stuck in anxiety and fear) or positively (by consistently taking action to improve your life).

It's clear that overthinking affects our lives very much. Is there a solution to this disease? In the next chapter, we will examine how to eliminate negative thinking and have that happy life you desire.

CHAPTER THREE

How to Eliminate Negative Thinking and Live Happily

"For God has not given us a spirit of timidity, but of power and love and discipline."

– 2 Timothy 1:7 (NKJV)

Lisa had reached the end of her rope. She was fed up with people telling her to stop being so negative as if she were being negative by choice.

Tom knew that his negativity was weighing him down, but hearing too many clichés like "life is what you make it" caused him to become even more anxious and cut himself off from the world completely.

The pandemic filled Jason with so much fear and negativity that he became agoraphobic and couldn't bring himself to leave the house.

Sammi had reached a point where she wasn't sure that life was worth fighting for, as every moment of her life seemed so bleak.

There are hundreds of thousands, if not millions, of people in the world today who are personally struggling with negativity. You're not alone. The problem with negativity is that it isn't simply a bad mood that you can shake off when you feel like it. Once rumination starts, the mind begins to dwell on only the negative aspects of a situation, and fear and anxiety take over.

We look for inspiration in the world, anything to shine a bit of light on our gloomy thoughts, but that doesn't happen. Over time, you start to notice more negative thinking going on than positive, like a sponge soaking up all the bad. Sadly, negative thinking can easily become a permanent state of mind that can wreak havoc on all areas of your life.

If you feel like you're walking on the very edge of a cliff and one more issue is likely to cause you to fall into a pit of depression and paralyzing fear, you aren't alone.

According to the National Science Foundation, 80% of our thoughts are negative (Kaida & Kaida, 2019). That is exhausting, to say the least. We are literally swimming in our negative thoughts, and many of us are drowning.

Negativity isn't like a broken leg or a skin rash. You can't see it, but you carry it around with you all the time. Not everyone can afford therapy or is comfortable with the idea of talking to a stranger about their innermost thoughts. Others are worried that they will be slapped with a mental illness label and just given antidepressants. So, how can you combat the negativity in order to bring happiness and joy back into your life?

Negative Thoughts

Negative thoughts are toxic to a healthy life and lead to deep unhappiness.

Thus, the first thing we have to gain control over is berating ourselves for our negative thought patterns. All those people who have told you that you're just a negative person and you aren't putting enough effort into being positive are wrong. Science tells us that our brain is trained to pay more attention to our negative thoughts. To an extent, there is a good reason for this.

When we are stressed or feeling scared, our brain releases cortisol and adrenaline hormones. These two hormones play a crucial role in the fight or flight response, which is a built-in biological response that protects us from danger. If your child starts crossing the street, for example, your first response is to grab their hand and probably shout at them because you fear an accident—even if no car is coming. Your brain and stress hormones are helping your body jump into action in order to protect you (or your loved ones). On the other hand, too much cortisol can have numerous consequences on our health. Some of these include:

- Weight gain
- Acne
- Thinning, easily-bruised skin
- Muscle weakness
- Severe fatigue
- High blood pressure
- Headaches

Increased blood pressure, headaches, weight gain, and severe anxiety are symptoms of too much adrenaline. This also puts you at greater risk of heart attacks and strokes. So, the release of cortisol and adrenaline is natural and is generally a good thing, but as soon as negative thinking becomes a severe issue, we are putting our health at risk.

There is another problem with an overactive fight or flight response. An increase in cortisol increases white matter in the brain. White matter is good for communication between the brain's gray matter, but it's the gray matter that carries out processes. Gray matter is necessary to cope with stress effectively. When white matter dominates and increases stress and fear, it becomes harder to decipher complex problems.

Those who don't suffer from negative thinking might be able to take a step back and view situations from alternative perspectives. In our heightened state of stress, this is much more difficult. Essentially, it is not your fault that your mind automatically jumps to negative conclusions.

We also have to consider that although our brain is an organ, it acts as a muscle: it needs training. Our brain has been trained in the wrong way through no fault of our own. Thanks to technology that scans the brain, we know that people who suffer from depression have an overdeveloped right prefrontal cortex, where negative thoughts are processed, and an underdeveloped left prefrontal cortex. Imagine lifting weights with only your right arm—your left will never be able to keep up. That's what happens to the brain when we continuously think negatively.

But as the brain is not a muscle, how does this actually work? The brain has approximately 100 billion neurons, and each neuron has an average of 7,000 synapses (connections to other neurons). All our negative thoughts and experiences get stored as memories. Every time we recall a memory, the synapses are strengthened. The more often these memories are accessed, the quicker and easier it is for negative thoughts to reappear.

Rewire Your Thought Process

Without wanting to bombard your mind with statistics, I feel it is crucial to help you understand how much stress affects us. Because we all seem to be under stress, it has almost become the norm rather than something that only occurs once in a while. In reality, our bodies aren't designed to cope with constant stress, and we are starting to see how damaging this is.

Some of the statistics below are shocking, but perhaps exactly what we need to help us realize that we have to start moving toward a less-stressed lifestyle.

- Americans between ages 30 and 49 are the most stressed.

- 52% of Generation Z has been diagnosed with mental health issues.

- 83% of U.S. workers suffer from work-related stress.

- 1 million individuals miss work every day because of stress.

- Depression costs companies $51 billion in absenteeism.

- Healthcare costs from stress cost $190 billion annually.

- Work-related stress causes 120,000 deaths in the U.S. each year.

(The American Institute of Stress, 2019)

We do not want to be a part of any of the above statistics! So, we must take control of stress and see it for what it is: fuel for unhappiness, negativity, and health problems and not something that we can afford to accept.

What the neuroscientists tell us

So, you're stressed out and feel like you're on the verge of exploding? Something has to give, and you don't want to cause a scene or breakdown. The good news is that there are four instant stress busters that you may or may not have heard of. The problem is because they are so simple, you might not feel they are powerful enough to work. For this reason, I have included neuroscience research to help convince you (Reeve & Lee, 2019).

1. Tense and relax your facial muscles

There is a communication loop between your brain and your body. When the gray matter in your brain creates stress, various muscles tense up. Once your muscles are tense, a message is sent back to the brain to let it know that the message has been received.

If you've tried asking your brain to stop stressing and it hasn't worked, you need to break the loop by making your body tell your brain that you are not stressed anymore. Consciously releasing the tension in your facial muscles sends that message. As you might imagine, the facial muscles are the best to use because they are more closely linked to our emotions. That being said, your hands, stomach, and, more surprisingly, your bum muscles will also send the right messages to the brain.

2. Do deep breathing

This may surprise you because we generally focus on the benefits of slow breathing, which can also be used to help reduce stress and feel calmer. But what about when we need to feel more excited, and get that adrenaline rush to work in our favor? Deep breathing (which is even used by Navy Seal recruits) activates the parasympathetic nervous system, necessary to conserve energy, and helps turn that stress into positive feelings.

3. Jolt your vagus nerve

The vagus nerve is the longest nerve in the body. It extends from the brain to the large intestine and is responsible for many critical body functions. In particular, it lowers heart rate and manages stress and anxiety. If this nerve is damaged, you may suffer from reduced attention and even depression.

Your vagus nerve is attached to your vocal cords. Therefore, singing or chanting can jolt your vagus nerve and offer some relief from stress. Alternatively, you can splash your face with cold water—a classic example of a traditional technique that you may have previously dismissed.

4. Listen to classical music

If you put on your all-time favorite tunes, you'll be tempted to sing, waking up the vagus nerve. But music can also help stress levels in other ways. Music engages a large part of the limbic system in the brain, which is responsible for our emotional responses. Music also increases heart rate (and, science aside, you know certain songs just make you feel better no matter what mood you're in!). Making music of your own, whether singing or playing an instrument, has an even more substantial effect on the limbic system.

Spiritual music can also ease your stress. In Samuel 16:14-23, we see music's therapeutic effect. When David plays the harp for King Saul, the king instantly feels better.

Next time you start to feel stress building up, remember these four highly effective brain tricks. Naturally, if you're in the middle of a meeting, you probably don't want to start making strange faces to release tension or burst out into song, but squeezing your bum muscles is a subtle alternative. You can also excuse yourself to the bathroom and splash your face with cold water to quickly alter your mindset. None of these solutions takes more than a couple of minutes.

Process of Negative Thoughts

Many people suffer from negative thoughts that sometimes turn into cognitive distortions. These are patterns of thinking that distort your view of reality and can have a detrimental effect on your psychological wellbeing.

No matter how great your life is, there will always be things you aren't happy with. This is normal. But if you let these thoughts get the better of you and they start causing real problems in your life, they need to be addressed. That's why it can be helpful to learn about them, so you're aware of when these patterns of thinking start popping up in your daily life. Here are some common negative thoughts and their distorted counterparts:

i. Jumping to conclusions

This is when you think a particular event means something it actually doesn't mean. You might create a very detailed scenario in your head of how something happened, often without checking for facts that could prove or disprove your assumptions. When you rush to conclusions and negatively interpret an event or circumstance based on a lack of evidence, you end up reacting to your false belief instead of the reality.

This distortion arises from the erroneous notion that we can read other people's mind and know their intentions. Of course, we can get a sense of what other people are thinking, but the distortion here pertains to the negative interpretations we make. When you jump to conclusions or attempt to "mind-read," it's usually in response to a persistent idea or concern. For instance, you may be anxious about your relationship or believe your partner is losing interest in you, and thus you always jump to the conclusion that he or she is being unfaithful.

ii. Catastrophizing

This is when you think something terrible is bound to happen when, realistically, the chances of such an event are really low. You might imagine a particular situation will end up very badly, (e.g., in death, divorce, or imprisonment).

When confronted with the unknown, this flawed thinking causes people to fear the worst. Common fears can suddenly increase when people catastrophize.

For example, let's say an expected check does not appear in the mail. Catastrophizing would lead you to conclude that it will never arrive and that, as a result, your family will be evicted from your home because you'll be unable to pay the rent. A more logical approach would be to assume that the check will show up in the next few days.

It's tempting for those who have not experienced it to dismiss catastrophizing as a hysterical overreaction; however, people who have developed this cognitive distortion may have been exposed to so many negative occurrences—such as chronic pain or childhood trauma— that they automatically fear the worst in various circumstances.

iii. Overgeneralization

Overgeneralization is a cognitive distortion involving believing that one event, or a single negative experience, reflects an entire category of people or events. Any negative experience can trigger this type of thinking, and it's very dangerous because it can make you feel so bad about the world around you that you become depressed or angry.

When people overgeneralize, they judge one occurrence and then apply that conclusion inappropriately to all situations. If you get a terrible score on one math test, for example, you might assume that you're just bad at math in general. Or if you have one traumatic relationship experience involving your partner cheating on you, you may come to believe that this is what will happen with all of your future relationships.

Post-traumatic stress disorder and other anxiety disorders have been linked to overgeneralization.

iv. Labeling

Labeling is a widespread cognitive distortion that all of us engage in to some extent. It is the process of defining oneself and others based on a particular trait, behavior, or event. Labeling someone in your mind can be both positive and negative. The harm of labeling occurs when people limit themselves or others to a single (generally negative) attribute or descriptor, such as "drunk" or "failure."

People can become self-critical as a result of being labeled. It can also lead to misinterpretation or underestimation of others by the thinker. This misunderstanding can lead to serious interpersonal issues. No one wants to be assigned a label.

v. "Should" statements

In general, "should" statements are used to manipulate others into doing what you want. They take the form of sentences like "You should have done this," or "you must" statements like "You must be a loser if you don't…"

A cognitive distortion is likely at work when people think only in terms of what "should" or "ought" to be said or done. It's rarely beneficial to berate yourself for not performing well at something you "should" be able to achieve. "Should" and "need" phrases are commonly used to adopt a negative picture of your life or the lives of others.

Internalized cultural or family expectations are often at the basis of these types of thoughts, which may or may not be suitable for your actual situation. Such beliefs can lower your self-esteem and increase your worry.

vi. *Emotional reasoning*

"I feel depressed, so it must be true that I'm a failure."

What's distorted about this thought is the assumption that what you feel is an accurate reflection of reality. Many people are unhappy when they're feeling unfulfilled in their lives. That dissatisfaction often reflects the gap between who you are and who you want to be, and thus is not a reflection of your real situation. Emotional reasoning is a thought pattern commonly fallen into by people with anxiety or depression (Howard, 2019).

Emotional reasoning is the delusion that your feelings are true—that how you feel about a situation is a trustworthy sign of reality. While listening to, affirming, and expressing your emotions is necessary, it's also critical to appraise reality based on facts.

vii. *Personalization and blame*

"It's my fault that I failed."
"It's my fault that they're upset."
"It's my fault that I've been single for so long."

The above statements are all examples of personalization. Personalization occurs when you assume full responsibility for an event even though other factors contributed to the outcome. If you suffer from personalization, you'll more than likely believe things such as "I'm a bad person" or "I'll never be successful." Alternatively, you may mistakenly believe you've been targeted or excluded by others on purpose.

Taking everything personally when it isn't associated with or influenced by you is one of the most common cognitive errors. If you frequently blame yourself for things that aren't your fault or are out of your control, you may be engaging in the personalization cognitive distortion. Personalization has been linked to increased anxiety and feelings of despair.

Replace Negative Thoughts with New Attitudes

The best way to alter a negative thought is to replace it with a positive one. The following techniques, based on a cognitive behavioral therapy (CBT) approach, can help you completely transform your outlook on life:

i. Ask yourself if the thought is realistic.

You must be able to recognize the error you're making in order to change an unproductive mental pattern.

Detecting the untrue ideas that cause your negative feelings and mindsets is crucial to resetting your cognitive processes.

It's also helpful to track when and where your thoughts appear. Certain settings may make you more susceptible to cognitive distortions. Knowing what those scenarios are will help you plan to avoid them ahead of time, or identify and correct the negative thought before it overwhelms you.

Some folks find that journaling as part of the process is beneficial. Writing down your thoughts can help you spot a cognitive distortion even if you're not sure what's causing your anxiety at first.

You'll likely notice skewed thought tendencies more quickly when you practice self-monitoring.

ii. Think of similar situations in the past and evaluate if your thoughts align with what took place.

Learning to examine your views and assumptions, particularly those which get in the way of leading a productive life, is an essential aspect of cognitive restructuring. This can help you discover how your unconscious thoughts are prejudiced or unreasonable.

Ask yourself the following questions:

- Is this a feeling or a fact-based thought?

- What proof do I have that this belief is correct?

- What evidence do I have that it's *incorrect*?

- How could I put this theory to the test?

- What are the worst-case scenarios? What would I do if anything terrible happened?

- How else can the data I'm receiving be interpreted?

- Is this a black-and-white situation, or are there shades of gray?

If you're suffering from the cognitive distortion known as catastrophizing (discussed above), you might be imagining the worst possible conclusion in a stressful circumstance. You could challenge this cognitive pattern by making a list of all conceivable outcomes and considering the likelihood of each scenario.

Questioning helps you evaluate alternate outcomes that aren't as disastrous as the ones you're afraid of.

iii. Actively challenge the thought and look for alternative explanations.

Gathering evidence is an important part of cognitive reorganization. You might want to keep track of the circumstances that cause a reaction in you, such as who you were with and what you were doing. Make note of how powerful each response was and what memories or fears were triggered as a result.

You should also try to acquire evidence to support or refute your ideas. Cognitive distortions are not only erroneous and biased, they're often profoundly ingrained in our mind. Challenging them and substituting them with other explanations will show you how irrational they are. You may also need to make a list of the facts (if any) that support your distorted belief and compare it against the facts that support an alternate belief.

If you suffer from the cognitive distortion of personalization, for example, you may tend to blame yourself for matters which aren't your fault. If you challenge this belief and consider the alternative—that you are not the cause of other people's behaviors—you may benefit greatly.

iv. *Think of what you gain versus what you lose by continuing to believe the thought.*

This method involves weighing the benefits and drawbacks of maintaining a cognitive distortion. Consider the following questions:

- What good does it do to believe I am unintelligent or incapable?

- What does this thought pattern cost me in terms of emotional distress and wasted time?

- What will be the long-term consequences of holding this belief?

- What impact does this mental pattern have on those around me?

- In what ways does it help or hinder my job performance?

Seeing the benefits and drawbacks side by side can help you decide whether changing the pattern is worthwhile (and it probably is!).

v. Recognize whether your thoughts are the result of a cognitive distortion.

The reason we benefit from cognitive restructuring is it allows us to see things in new ways. Part of the technique entails recognizing the cognitive distortion you're falling prey to and then coming up with rational, constructive alternative explanations to replace the distortions that have become entrenched over time.

Let's say you didn't do well on a math test and you start thinking that you're just terrible at math (overgeneralizing) and you're going to fail out of school (catastrophizing). You then catch yourself, identify these two patterns of cognitive distortion, and decide to look into ways to improve your study habits instead of continuing the negative thought process.

Another example: A group of coworkers stops chatting when you enter the room. Immediately, you think to yourself, "They must have been talking about me. I must've done something wrong." Once you realize that you've fallen into the trap of several distortions (including jumping to conclusions and personalization), you start thinking about other possible reasons that your coworkers stopped talking. You may discover that it had nothing to do with you or that you misread what was going on.

Develop Endurance

Endurance can be defined as the body's ability to function for extended periods of time without becoming exhausted. For example, if you're able to run a long distance, such as running a marathon, you have good physical endurance.

We need more than just physical endurance in this life, however. It presents many challenges, and you need mental, emotional, and spiritual endurance to get through them. Think of your life as a sailboat on the ocean. You will face storms. Certain circumstances or news will shake you to your very core. You have to set your mind to stay strong, no matter the situation. You have to develop endurance to succeed.

You don't have much control over what happens to you, but you *can* control how to react to each situation. Your state of mind will determine your reaction. In the first century AD, the Stoic philosopher Seneca wrote: "Fire tests gold, suffering tests brave men." Problems, and yes, suffering, will come to test you. No huge tree can become profoundly rooted in the ground if strong winds do not blast against it. Your adversities and your suffering will strengthen your tree by allowing it to plant its roots deeper into the ground, and will ultimately make you stronger—if you put your faith more deeply in Jesus.

In the situation you are in right now, ask God to help develop your endurance. Do not let anger take over your emotions. Remember what scripture tells us about going through challenging times: "And not only that, but we also glory in tribulations, knowing that tribulation produces perseverance; and perseverance, character; and character, hope." (Romans 5:3-4, NKJV)

No matter what you are going through, focus on your goals and focus on God, and He will help you to weather the storm.

Become Unbreakable

In the Bible, God said, "Send men to spy out the land of Canaan, which I am giving to the children of Israel; from each tribe of their fathers, you shall send a man, every one a leader among them." (Numbers 13:2, NKJV) After receiving this command from the Lord, twelve spies went to the borders of Canaan territory to explore and examine the region.

Ten of the twelve (all except Joshua and Caleb) had negative thinking. They said things like:

- The people of Canaan are more powerful than Israel. (Verse 28)

- We are not able to go up against the people, for they are stronger than we. (Verse 31)

- The land through which we have gone as spies is a land that devours its inhabitants. (Verse 32)

- All the people whom we saw in it are men of great stature. (Verse 32)

- There we saw the giants (the descendants of Anak came from the giants), and we were like grasshoppers in our own sight, and so we were in their sight. (Verse 33)

These ten spies gave multiple reasons why they could not go and take Canaan. Because of the ten spies' negative thinking, they and the people of Israel (except Joshua and Caleb) did not enter Canaan. Even though God said He had given this land to Israel (Numbers 13:2), the spies' negative thinking messed up God's plan. They forgot all that God had done for them in the past. They certainly had to face many obstacles, but the only thing they had to do in order to succeed was move forward with faith, relying on God's promises.

This story shows us that people who dwell in negative thinking forget or deny God's promises. Your negative thinking can destroy God's plan for your life, and your influence can be disastrous for others. You are better than that. Let's face our battles with faith.

Like the ten spies, the stressful situations in your life may feel like huge giants before you. The challenges may seem like way more than you can handle. But with the help of God Almighty, no battle is too difficult for you. Face your challenges with faith; He brought you this far, and He will not fail you here.

Perspective is everything.

When faced with the same situation as the ten spies who did not trust in God, Caleb said, "Let us go up at once and take possession, for we are well able to overcome it" (Numbers 13:30). It's about time to be like Joshua and Caleb. You can face any challenge with God's help.

Ask the Lord to remove your negative thinking from your mind. Despite your giants, your future is bright in Jesus. God says to you:

"For I know the thoughts that I think toward you says the Lord, thoughts of peace and not of evil, to give you a future and a hope."

– Jeremiah 29:11 (NKJV)

With Jesus, you are unbreakable. Paul writes:

"Yet in all these things we are more than conquerors through Him who loved us."

– Romans 8:37 (NKJV)

Key Takeaways

- The first step toward change is becoming aware of the situation, recognizing your cognitive distortions, and developing endurance through difficulties.

- Making positive changes to your life can be challenging, but it is also very rewarding. Keep going forward, and do not get discouraged by the small setbacks you may experience along the way.

If you stay dedicated and determined, there is no reason you cannot achieve the results you want and deserve in life.

- Remind yourself that with God, you are unbreakable. You should be proud of how far you've progressed in your journey with this book.

Time to Take Action

Negative thinking is a cycle that can be broken with hard work, commitment, and lots of practice. You don't need to suffer with the negative thoughts, stress, and anxiety forever; you can change and reframe these patterns. In this chapter, you have learned to identify and understand your negative thinking patterns, transform them into more positive ways of thinking, and utilize some coping techniques to manage the worries and anxieties that can result from your thoughts and feelings.

What's more, you have hopefully learned how to see the joy in your life once again and how to find the little things that make you happy. However, the work is not over. It is essential to keep going with these techniques, as change takes time and does not happen overnight.

Permanent changes require gradual and consistent steps to ensure they are cemented in your new mindset. Do not be tempted to rush, as you're only at the beginning of a long but extremely rewarding journey.

With time and patience, you can achieve all the goals you've set out to achieve and ensure that you reap the rewards of your hard work. As you continue along your path, you'll notice many significant areas of your life begin to improve.

Put your faith in God. With His help, you will be victorious.

Mental clarity is all it takes—but how do you develop mental clarity? The next chapter will help you dissect this concept and open up your mind to have a better understanding of your next steps.

CHAPTER FOUR

How to Develop Mental Clarity in a Noisy World

"For I know the plans I have for you, declares the LORD, plans for welfare and not for evil, to give you a future and a hope."

– Jeremiah 29:11(NIV)

Nat's brain fog dilemma

Let's look at another story to see an example of how to develop mental clarity.

It was what felt like just another day at the office as Nat sat at her desk, staring at her computer screen but unable to concentrate on what she was looking at.

"Nat, is everything okay?" Luke, one of her colleagues, asked.

They had been working together in the data analysis office for a few years, so Luke knew it wasn't usual for Nat to be stuck on a project. She was one of the best because she was always so focused and usually got the best and most important projects and clients.

"I just can't seem to concentrate on this project," Nat replied with a worried look. "I'm not sure what I'm trying to do. It almost feels like my mind is clouded, and I'm just so tired…" She yawned before she continued, "I'd better go make a coffee. Do you want one?"

Luke shook his head and stopped Nat with an extended hand.

"Nat, I don't think coffee is the answer. I know how stressed and anxious you've been lately with the new workload, and I think what you need is to clear your mind."

"To clear my mind?" Nat looked skeptical.

"Yes. I've been where you are. I'm a massive overthinker, and it caused so many problems for me that I now work on developing mental clarity every day. Do you want some advice?"

"Sure, anything to get rid of this brain fog," Nat said as she sat down again.

"One of the best things you can do is to make sure you're sleeping enough and getting the rest you need.

Track your sleep if you need to, but make sure you're sleeping about eight hours every night. You've got to work on your nutrition too, and make sure your body is well-nourished. Eat balanced meals, and drink plenty of water throughout the day. And finally, work on the things that generate anxiety for you to make sure they don't overwhelm you. If you do all that, your mind will start to clear up again."

Nat thanked Luke for the advice, and that night, she started planning her sleep schedule as well as a new nutrition plan. She knew her mind wasn't the way she'd like it to be, and she understood now that she needed to put in the work to make sure things got better. Luke was right; her mind hadn't been clear, and she had to turn the situation around.

If you're interested in cognitive development, self-improvement, or just want to sharpen your mind a little, this section is for you.

We'll dig into what mental clarity is and provide a variety of ways to increase it. We'll also look at the different types of brain fog and detail their causes and effects.

Mental Clarity

Mental clarity is a feeling of deep focus, knowledge, or wisdom. It doesn't refer to the absence of mental illness, but rather the ability to be mentally stable and to focus on what you're doing. Someone who has clarity can typically think more clearly and make good decisions. They are also better at understanding themselves and others. Clarity is a trait that is often desired by people who are depressed or stressed, as they tend to suffer from brain fog.

Some people describe clarity as an elevated state of being. It's often associated with other terms such as focus, empowerment, mindfulness, and even inspiration. Clarity can be achieved in many ways, and it's often dependent on a person's specific needs. Some methods are more effective than others for achieving it, but regardless, achieving clarity requires a certain mindset. So, you're probably wondering what exactly goes into achieving this mental state.

In order to achieve mental clarity, you must have an open mind, a positive attitude, and confidence. You should be curious about the world around you and learn how things work.

Are You Lacking Mental Clarity?

Your brain is an amazing organ. It's responsible for thinking and making decisions and controlling emotions like fear and happiness. It's also a storage facility for our memories, thoughts, and dreams. However, sometimes stress and other factors can bog down the brain and dampen a person's mental clarity.

If you've ever felt lost and confused or felt like life is passing you by, it may be time to check your mental clarity. Does your mind frequently wander, and do you leave tasks half-done, or not done at all? Do you experience brain fog, a feeling of "fuzziness" inside your head that prevents you from thinking clearly?

Here are some of the signs that you're experiencing a lack of mental clarity:

i. Inability to focus or concentrate

Mental clarity is the ability to stay on task and in the moment. It requires that you hold your attention on something for extended periods of time. An inability to focus over an extended period of time can indicate that you might lack mental clarity.

Concentration occurs naturally and without effort when we are mentally healthy. Pay attention to how much work it takes you to concentrate. This can offer an indication of how powerful your current mental state is.

ii. *Physical or mental exhaustion*

If you're experiencing physical or mental fatigue, it could signify that you lack mental clarity. Exhaustion is often caused by poor diet, lack of sleep, and stress. When the energetic resources of our minds are drained, the rest of the body generally follows suit.

Physical and mental exhaustion are possible side effects of low mental clarity, and they may indicate that it's time to make a behavioral change. A lack of mental clarity may well be the cause of you feeling tired and lethargic after even the simplest tasks.

iii. *Loss of interest and lack of motivation*

Lack of motivation can also be a sign of a lack of mental clarity. If you lack initiative, you're likely to have low energy, feel unmotivated, and have low self-esteem.

Another sign of low mental clarity is a loss of interest in things or tasks that used to offer you joy. When our minds are clear and powerful, we have a natural desire to study. Your lack of motivation could indicate that your mind is in need of rejuvenation.

iv. Memory problems

Memory problems can also be a symptom of low mental clarity. You might find yourself misplacing things, having trouble remembering names and numbers, or unable to recall events. Poor memory recall is a clear symptom of low mental performance, just as a great ability to recollect memories is a sign of excellent mental performance.

Memory retention should never be an issue when our thoughts are healthy and clear. Checking the sharpness of your memory recall is a wonderful approach to keeping track of your mental health.

Causes of Decreased Mental Clarity

Before we can understand how to improve mental clarity, we must first examine the possible causes or triggers that affect it. These factors exhaust our mental resources, making mental performance considerably more difficult. If any of these seem familiar, you've probably figured out what's to blame.

i. Lack of sleep

Have you ever woken up feeling unprepared for the day? A lack of sleep can also cause lack of mental clarity, as you're less alert and your brain isn't functioning smoothly. You might find your ability to think and your focus diminished after a sleepless night. This can in turn lead to excessive caffeine or sugar consumption in an attempt to keep the brain alert, which only creates more mental fog.

An excellent circadian rhythm is an essential component of human health. The mind and body struggle to work at their best when you don't get seven or more hours of sleep each night.

Some of us have trouble sleeping because of stress, while others have poor sleep hygiene. People who work irregular hours are at higher risk of developing sleep disorders. You may be jeopardizing your mental health if you do not give your body the rest it needs.

ii. Stress and anxiety

Stress is probably the most common cause of mental fog. Stress can cause your mind to shut down to protect itself from the demands you place on it. It also makes it difficult to process information and make decisions. We are all aware that stress is harmful to our health (although sometimes a little stress can be a good motivator), but it can also be a powerful mental foe.

High cortisol levels are a result of chronic stress, which signifies decreased circulation—and poor circulation causes your heart to send less oxygen to your brain. This might lead to a loss of mental clarity, which can exacerbate your stress and worry. If left untreated, it can become a vicious cycle.

iii. Poor nutrition

Another major cause of mental fog is poor nutrition. The nutrients in the foods you eat affect your brain, behavior, and even how you feel. Your brain needs essential fatty acids, vitamin B, vitamin C, and vitamin E that are found in nuts and vegetables.

There are a variety of foods that can help you focus and think clearly, but many of us have poor nutrition due to a lack of variety in our diet or a high intake of processed foods. Too little or the wrong kinds of nutrients can cause brain fog and low mental clarity. A poor diet can also cause a lack of nutrition. It's hard to think clearly when blood sugar levels aren't regulated and nutrients aren't absorbed properly by the body.

Vitamin B-12, in particular, offers numerous brain and immune system benefits. Fish, meat, poultry, eggs, and dairy products all contain this vitamin. Omega-3 fatty acids and other healthy fats also benefit the brain, particularly when it comes to minor memory loss and depression. (But remember to consume in moderation! You can have too much of a good thing. Consume too much of omega-3 or vitamin B, and you could have negative effects like mental fuzziness, headaches and maybe even nausea.)

Importance of Mental Clarity

Mental clarity is essential because it offers us a sense of empowerment and helps us to function in the world. Mental clarity is greatly affected by our physical health: what we eat, how much we exercise, and how well we sleep all impacts how our mind works on a daily basis.

When you don't have mental clarity, it's tough to enjoy your life and be productive because you can't make good decisions, stick to your plans, or work towards fulfilling the goals you've set for yourself. Both in and out of the office, mental clarity is essential for productivity and fulfillment. To solve problems and stay on top of whatever obstacles come our way, we need a clear mind.

So, how can mental clarity help you achieve your personal and professional objectives? Let's have a look.

i. Helps you make better decisions

Mental clarity helps you think more clearly, which in turn will improve your decision-making skills. When you're mentally clear and focused, you can see things from different perspectives and make choices that are in your own and other people's best interests. You'll also be better at evaluating situations and problem-solving.

A cloudy mind leads to cloudy judgment. If you want to make good decisions in life, you need to have good judgment.

ii. Helps you find focus and direction

If you have poor mental clarity, you're more likely to get distracted by the irrelevant and the trivial. You'll also find it harder to stay focused, which can cause unanticipated consequences. If your mind is cluttered with thoughts, memories, and experiences, it will be harder to focus. Clarity of the mind will help you think more clearly and focus on the task at hand.

iii. Makes it easier to organize tasks and prioritize

When your mind is clear, you'll be more likely to feel in control of your life and be able to live it in the best way possible. This will make it easier for you to organize tasks and prioritize. "A crowded desk is a symptom of a cluttered mind," as the old saying goes.

Organizing becomes second nature when your mind is operating at peak performance. A well-organized mind can approach things more efficiently and complete them in the sequence in which they were assigned.

iv. Helps you enjoy life more

Being able to focus, make good decisions, organize your thoughts efficiently, and stick to your plans helps you to enjoy life more. Lack of mental clarity can make you feel confused and uncertain about what you should do next. When your mind is clear, it will be easier for you to make the right choices and feel in control of your life. With mental clarity, you'll get more out of life in terms of purpose and happiness.

We can perceive life more clearly and prioritize what's most essential to us when we have mental clarity. This includes spending quality time with family and friends as well as pursuing personal development.

Improving Your Mental Clarity for Personal Growth

When your mental state is clear, you'll be able to process information more effectively and make better decisions. You might find it easier to identify problems and come up with solutions that work for you. Your ability to be productive will improve and you'll enjoy life more.

Meditation and prayer can help to improve your mental clarity in the long term by clearing out the clutter and making way for positive thoughts and experiences.

In short, mental clarity is at the heart of health, productivity, and performance, regardless of where you are in life, and your own mental clarity contributes to the clarity of those around you, whether at work or within your family.

Taking care of your mental health is an important aspect of living a happy and whole life. There are numerous straightforward techniques to develop mental clarity for personal growth and success in whatever endeavor you set your mind to, as we've learned.

What happens if your head is unclear?

When you don't have mental clarity, even the simplest things become difficult. Low mental performance can manifest itself in a variety of ways, both in the body and in the mind.

i. Struggling to perform well at work

When your mind is foggy, one of the first things to suffer is your work performance. Because employment necessitates mental acuity, a lack of clarity will make work more difficult than it needs to be. If your work performance standards are slipping, it's possible that you're coping with a muddled mind.

ii. Isolation and detachment from loved ones

Your emotional wellbeing influences your mental clarity. Many people with poor mental clarity experience feelings of loneliness or isolation. This occurs as a natural self-preservation mechanism. You waste less mental energy on maintaining relationships when there are fewer people around you.

iii. Depression and low self-esteem

A combination of low mental energy, poor job performance, and isolation from friends and family can swiftly lead to mental illness.

When you know you aren't performing at your best, it might be difficult to see yourself in a good light. As a result, you're more likely to develop self-doubt, low self-esteem, and even imposter syndrome. If not handled, this can lead to depression.

iv. Sleep disturbances

Sleep deprivation and mental stress are very closely associated. When you're anxious, it's likely you'll have difficulty sleeping, which only contributes to more stress.

Your sleep schedule is influenced by your mental acuity. You may find that you're sleeping too little or too much if your mental health is suffering. This can cause brain fog in a variety of ways.

Your natural circadian rhythm, or your internal body clock, is disrupted by poor sleep hygiene, such as irregular sleep and wake times, having fewer than seven to eight hours of sleep per night, or blue light exposure before bed.

Blue light reduces the melatonin hormone required for deep REM sleep, and to consolidate and integrate memories from the day, both REM and non-REM sleep are needed. Additionally, because your body and brain detox the most between the hours of 10 p.m. and 2 a.m., staying awake during this time disrupts the body's natural detoxification process and can contribute to mental fogginess.

An early morning wake time that does not coincide with the end of a sleep cycle can also impair cognitive performance and make you feel sleepy and foggy during the day. One way to deal with this is to download an app like Sleep Cycle, which tracks your movement throughout the night to determine what stage of sleep you're in. Then, it sets your alarm to go off at the end of your sleep cycle, ensuring you don't wake up in the middle of a cycle. Note also that pushing the snooze button after your alarm goes off will not help you feel more rested; instead, it will increase your chances of falling asleep and being awakened once again.

How to Develop Mental Clarity

Despite the difficulties you may experience if you have poor mental clarity, there are a variety of strategies you can employ to encourage attentive engagement. You have the power to make things better for yourself.

These eight mental clarity methods are all simple to include in your everyday routine. They can aid in the development of a keen, active, and clear mind.

1. Get plenty of restful sleep.

The amount of sleep you get determines how much energy you have during the day. Both mental and physical energy are affected by this. You must prevent generating a backlog of fatigue (or "sleep debt") and ensure that your mental performance is on point all day long by maintaining a consistent and healthy sleep routine. One approach to ensuring you get adequate, quality sleep is to use a sleep tracker.

2. Take control of your tension.

Knowing how to successfully manage stress levels will have a significant impact on your mental clarity. Finding individualized tension release and relaxation strategies is an important part of stress management. You can also use a stress tracker device to keep track of your stress levels throughout the day. Being conscious of your stress levels will help you maintain mental sharpness and achieve your best potential.

3. Develop a mindfulness practice.

Mindfulness is the attitude of living in the present moment. You can better regulate your energy by slowing down and being aware of your body, environment, and activities.

4. Strike an excellent work-life balance.

Work-life balance entails making time for both work and recreation. You may drain your energy levels and experience burnout if you spend too much time at the office. Similarly, if you concentrate solely on relaxing and having fun, you'll get very little done and be unable to achieve your goals. Knowing how to improve mental clarity requires striking a healthy balance between the two.

5. Take care of yourself.

Self-care is an essential part of life. You can control your stress levels and stay productive by finding the activities, settings, and people that make you feel comfortable and supported. Taking time out of your week to do something that brings you joy is beneficial to your mental health. It will also help you maintain a flexible and robust mindset.

6. Get your body moving.

Moving your body regularly is an essential component of overall health, both emotionally and physically. Sweating out impurities and activating the circulatory system can keep your mind busy. Even simple exercises such as walking or swimming might help you achieve mental clarity.

7. Eat a balanced diet.

That's right—you can actually eat your way to a sharper mind. Nutrition and mental health are inextricably intertwined, which is why eating a balanced diet is so critical for general wellness. Many foods can provide you with all of the nutrients you require to cultivate mental vigor.

8. Seek assistance.

Many people find it difficult to seek out help when they're going through a difficult period. However, asking for help is one of the most self-empowering things a person can do. It's not uncommon to get stressed out by mental fogginess. Ask for help from friends, family, or a healthcare professional if you need it. They will make you feel acknowledged and understood.

9. Seek God daily.

A daily encounter with God in prayer will help you. He has the power to give you all the mental clarity you require.

I remember a time when I was in my late twenties; I was in a confusing situation. I did not have the clarity of mind necessary to make a significant decision. One day, I was in a meeting with some pastors. One of them gave me a text that would change my life forever:

"I will instruct you and teach you in the way you should go; I will guide you with My eye. Do not be like the horse or like the mule, Which have no understanding, Which must be harnessed with bit and bridle, Else they will not come near you."

– Psalm 32:8-9 (NKJV)

God promises to instruct you, teach you, and guide you. With God's help, you will receive the mental clarity you need to navigate any confusing situation.

Key Takeaways

- Mental clarity comes from the development and maintenance of certain mental, emotional, cognitive, and spiritual traits. A lack of mental clarity may be due to stress, poor sleep, or poor nutrition, and can affect work performance, relationships, and mental health.

- Improving your mental clarity will ultimately make you happier, more organized, and more fulfilled.

- Understanding the advantages of mental clarity allows us to improve our own lives by sharpening our brain's performance through good sleep, diet, exercise, and spiritual practices.

- An increased capacity for mental clarity results in significant personal growth, both professionally and in your everyday life.

- Seek God daily and ask Him to give you the mental clarity you need.

Time to Take Action

Overwhelming thoughts are some of the most significant barriers to personal growth. We all have moments where we overthink or worry about something instead of taking action. These habits are often detrimental to our mental clarity, emotional wellbeing, and sense of fulfillment.

Be mindful of your thoughts. Take note of the types of thoughts that are passing through your mind throughout the day. Are they clear? Are they rational? Or are they foggy and vague? You might even consider writing down some of these thoughts. This exercise is beneficial because it allows you to be accountable to yourself and understand clearly which thought patterns are not supportive of your aims. Realize that not every thought you have is important or should be taken seriously, and then use the tips in this chapter to improve your mental clarity.

Once you've opened the door to mental clarity, the next step is stress management. What are the sources of stress, and what can you do to manage it? The next chapter will guide you on the journey of stress management.

CHAPTER FIVE

Steps for Personal Stress Management

"You shall not fear them, for it is the LORD your God who fights for you."

– Deuteronomy 3:22 (NKJV)

Lucy's therapy session

This short story will give you an example of everyday stressors and how to manage them:

"I don't know what to do," Lucy said to her therapist as tears streamed down her cheeks. There were so many things on her plate right now that she didn't know where to start.

"First, take a deep breath with me," Ms. Peters said. "Now, let's list the things that are stressing you out, okay?"

"Well, to start, I have three exams coming up in the next two weeks. Then I need to finish a lab report, and my mom is organizing a party that she keeps insisting she needs help with. Also, Alan is complaining that it's been a while since we hung out and says I don't give him enough time. But I don't *have* time!" Lucy cried.

"Okay, okay, breathe," Ms. Peters said softly. Lucy took a deep breath and waited for her therapist's wisdom.

"There are two things I want you to do. First, organize those tasks in order of urgency. Which one needs to be done first? Then organize them in order of importance. Some might be both important and urgent, while some might be important but not under a tight deadline. Also, Alan needs to understand that sometimes you're going to be busy and have less time for him. It's important that through it all, you make time for yourself. You can't make other people your priority. *You* have to be your priority, okay?"

Lucy nodded.

"Write things down," added Ms. Peters. "Write what you need to do, your top priority, and then just do it. Also, pay attention to which of those things stresses you out the most, as you might want to get those out of the way faster too. And finally, when you're doing one of those tasks, forget about the rest. The moment you pick a task, that task is all that matters, okay?"

"Okay," Lucy replied, feeling a little bit more hopeful with a plan in sight.

This story brings out several aspects of stress. We'll discuss how to tackle them in detail—but first, we need an understanding of the sources of stress.

Sources of Stress

There are four primary sources of stress in our lives:

1. **Environmental:** The environment can present you with a barrage of competing demands. Weather, noise, crowds, pollution, traffic, dangerous and poor housing, and crime are all examples of environmental stressors.

2. **Social:** The pressures of our various social responsibilities, such as being a parent, spouse, caregiver, and employee, can cause us to suffer from stress. Deadlines, financial troubles, job interviews, presentations, conflicts, demands for your time and attention, loss of a loved one, divorce, and co-parenting are all instances of social stressors.

3. **Physiological:** Physiological stresses are circumstances that affect our bodies. Adolescence, menopause, disease, aging, giving birth, accidents, lack of exercise, poor nutrition, and sleep disorders are all examples of physiological stressors.

4. **Mental:** Your brain classifies situations as stressful, challenging, painful, or enjoyable. Some life situations are stressful, but oftentimes our thoughts determine whether or not they are an issue for us.

Tackle the Common Stressors

Stress is a common part of life, and it may help you get things done. Even extreme stress caused by serious disease, job loss, a family tragedy, or a traumatic life event can be normal. You may feel depressed or anxious for a period, which is natural, and then begin to recover. If you're feeling low or nervous for more than a few weeks, however, or if it's interfering with your home or work life, check with your doctor. Therapy, medicine, and other approaches may be beneficial.

Stress can be a healthy reaction to a given situation, but it can also become a problem if it affects your everyday activities. Excessive stress can interfere with your health as well as your relationships. So, how do you properly manage your stress, and what are the best ways to avoid it? Keep reading to find out!

Academics and work

The first thing you should do is try to harmonize your personal life with your academic and/or work responsibilities. Try to plan out a schedule that fits these different aspects of your life. You should have a set time for homework or answering emails, a set time to go to bed at night, etc. This will help you organize your time and feel more balanced. Avoid rushing through school or work tasks; block out enough time in your day so that you can complete them comfortably. Stick to your schedule as much as you can to avoid getting stressed out by tasks piling up.

Time and task management

Time management is key to stress control. If you don't effectively manage your time and priorities, you can easily become overwhelmed. People frequently experience stress when they believe they are running out of time to finish a task. Simple time management practices might help you feel more comfortable and focused. So, how do you manage your time properly?

First, make a list of everything that is important and needs to be completed. These are usually your daily or weekly responsibilities. Once you have created this list, prioritize the items from most to least important. Then, try to complete these items one at a time in order of priority. Be sure to tackle the essential things first, then work your way down the list. This will help you feel more accomplished throughout your day.

In addition, create a timeframe within which to accomplish these tasks. For example, if it is a one-hour task, plan on spending one hour on this particular activity; once the period is over, reward yourself and take a break! This will help you stay motivated and organized throughout your regular activities.

Consider developing a written timetable, segmenting your duties into reasonable time periods, planning accordingly, and scheduling time for relaxation or socializing each day. Divide your job into critical versus unimportant tasks, as well as urgent versus non-urgent.

Look on the bright side

One of the best ways to reduce stress is to accept it and look at the good things in your life. Focusing on the positives can help you relax by diverting your attention away from your unpleasant thoughts or releasing built-up tension. When you are stressed out and frustrated, think about what's working for you now instead of the negative aspects. For example, don't think about the fact that you cracked your phone screen and were late to pick up your child from school; instead, think about how lucky you are to have a smartphone and how much your child makes you laugh.

You can also try to look at things from a positive perspective by optimistically visualizing them. For example, imagine you're going to the beach for vacation. When you get there and look out over the horizon, instead of looking at all the bad parts of this beach, just look at the beautiful waves and the glittering white sand. This will make you feel much more relaxed and excited.

If you feel stressed over school or work, think about positive outcomes for the things stressing you out. For example, if you're stressed about an upcoming exam, think of how confident you'll feel when graduation day finally comes. Or, if a particular part of your job is making you frustrated, remember the positive aspects of your job that make it worth doing at the end of the day.

Exercise

Going for a walk or run can be very effective in reducing stress. Not only will it help you to feel much less stressed, but it will also give you time to think about how to handle your problems logically and rationally. Running will help you to clear your head and get rid of all the distractions that stress brings.

If you have time to work out for an extended period, try doing a high-intensity circuit training workout. This kind of exercise is perfect because it encourages the release of endorphins, which are feel-good neurotransmitters that are released in the brain while exercising. These endorphins can give a natural feeling of euphoria or relaxation. This type of high-intensity exercise also demands your attention, which can distract you from your fears and anxieties.

Relax

Learning relaxation techniques can assist you in dealing with both mental and physical fears. Simply lowering your shoulders and inhaling deeply, then exhaling slowly can help. Consider imagining yourself in a relaxed environment, like a beach, as described above.

Eat healthily

Eat a lot of fruits and vegetables, good proteins, healthy fats and whole grains, and limit your sugar intake. If you eat too much sugar (or drink sugary beverages), the resulting drop in your blood sugar can make you feel anxious. Caffeine can also increase anxiety levels, so if possible, consider reducing your caffeine intake as well.

Avoid alcohol

Some people call alcohol "liquid courage," but the after-effects of alcohol can make you feel even more afraid or anxious. Thus, it's probably best to use other strategies when you're feeling anxious at a social event rather than relying on alcohol to get you through.

Turn to God in prayer

God can help you through any stressful situation. Nothing is too complicated for Him to handle. He is good, and He wants the best for you. God said in His Word, "The Lord will fight for you, and you shall hold your peace" (Exodus 14:14, NKJV). God will fight for you in your anxious situation.

And Jesus tells us:

"Come to Me, all you who labor and are heavily laden, and I will give you rest."

– Matthew 11:28 (NKJV)

Key Takeaways

- Try to control your stress by managing your schedule and setting priorities.

- If you're having trouble dealing with stress, take things one at a time, focusing on the most important projects first.

- Learn how to enjoy life and look on the bright side. Seeking the positive moments in your day will help you to relax.

- Pay attention to how you're eating and try to incorporate daily exercise to keep yourself healthy and strong. A healthy body will contribute to a healthy mind.

- Exercise can help you feel less stressed and soothe your nerves. Try to walk or jog as much as possible, even if only for a short time each day. You don't need to go for long distances at a time.

- Remember, God wants to fight for you. Ask Him for help and you will receive it.

Time to Take Action

Stress is a regular and valuable part of life. It helps us cope with dangerous or frightening situations and allows us to react appropriately in these situations. However, if you're feeling stressed for long periods, it can be dangerous for your health and lead to physical and mental problems.

If you've been feeling stressed lately, consider trying one or all of the following strategies:

- Take some time off from work
- Consider clinical therapy

- Improve your diet by incorporating a balanced variety of healthy foods

- Make exercise part of your daily routine, even if only for 10 minutes

- Incorporate prayer into all aspects of your day

In the next chapter, we will discuss how to maintain a balanced life and achieve relief from fear and anxiety.

CHAPTER SIX

A Balanced Life Will Give You Relief

"Be diligent to present yourself approved to God, a worker who does not need to be ashamed, rightly dividing the word of truth."

– 2 Timothy 2:15 (NKJV)

Jim's desk

Let's look at an example of how decluttering your environment in your everyday life can give you relief from stress and anxiety:

Jim was sitting at his messy desk, trying to finish up a work project, but his mind was all over the place. His empty coffee mug was calling for him to wash it, the pile of papers he still hadn't graded seemed to be mocking him, and the various objects scattered around and collecting dust were just a reminder that he still hadn't gotten around to deep cleaning the house.

He tried to type something and then got distracted by another tab he had opened. He watched a YouTube video for a few minutes before realizing he wasn't even attempting to work anymore.

Twenty minutes passed like this, with Jim coming back to the file and getting distracted again. In all that time, the file remained unchanged. Jim simply couldn't concentrate. Finally deciding to do something about it, he got up. He took the coffee mug to the kitchen, washed it, and put it away, then put the ungraded papers in a drawer with a note stating the deadline. He also cleaned up all the little trinkets and things scattered around the wooden desk surface. After that, he wiped the desk and made sure there wasn't anything in his line of sight that could distract him. He left only his computer, a notepad, and a pen on the desk.

Finally, content with how things were looking, he sat back down and re-opened the file. Before he started working, though, he closed all the other tabs and windows on the computer, decluttering his screen as well as the physical space in which he was working. He knew all those things could distract him too, and he needed to be rid of them.

And so, with a clear space and a clear mind, Jim began his work.

Jim hadn't realized that the clutter and mess around him was the one thing distracting him from what he was supposed to be doing. But eventually, it clicked, and he tidied up his space before tackling the important tasks. Getting rid of the clutter made him more proactive and productive because fewer things could distract him. All the unnecessary things around him were merely sources of worry that caused Jim to overthink about the other things he had to do, so getting rid of them logically got rid of the problem too.

Like Jim, you probably have a lot of things that are cluttering your life. Many of us have things to do that cause mental clutter. Every day, there are new fires to put out, and it's easy to push the panic button as we worry about what we're going to do. Worrying, however, does not help things but instead makes them worse. The important thing we need to focus on is dealing with our mental clutter because that is the way we can go forward with our lives. But before we do that, we need to discover how mental clutter affects us in the first place.

What Is Mental Clutter?

Mental clutter includes anything that enters our lives that causes us to feel burdened or flustered. It consists of the things on our to-do list, regrets over things we've done in the past, unfinished work, messages to be sent, and bills to be paid, among other things. We tend to worry about many things, even if we don't know whether or not they'll happen. Worrying, being anxious, and even complaining can also be sources of mental clutter. Finally, perfectionism affects our ability to move forward because we fear failure, and thus it can contribute to mental clutter as well.

Once you're able to identify the sources of your mental clutter, what can you do about it?

Define Your Core Values

When you stay focused on your core values, you'll be able to clear up the mental clutter and pursue your most important goals. For some people, faith or religion defines their core values. For others, personal freedom might be their number one value, as they believe that restrictions on these things will cause more harm than good. For others, the importance of family may supersede all other considerations.

For me, the most important thing I believe in is Jesus and His teachings. If you are also a person of faith, it will be fairly easy to define your core values based on the principles found in the Bible.

Why are core values so important?

Much of modern life is busy and hectic, with people doing more than they can take on, resulting in excessive stress. When we add too much to our to-do list, we often stress more because we don't think we'll be able to get everything done. But when we focus on the important things in light of our core values, we can lighten our loads and free ourselves of the unnecessary mental clutter. Try to ease the burdens currently in your life by taking on fewer tasks. This will enable you to do a lot more and be more efficient.

Get rid of physical clutter to reduce mental clutter

Nowadays, our homes are filled with things we never use—books we don't read, DVDs we'll never watch again, gadgets picking up dust, clothes we never wear. Even our email inboxes are filled with unread messages, and our phones continually alert us that we're running low on storage space.

As we fill our homes with more things than we need, we also clutter our minds with more stress. Information is all around us, but we don't know how to handle all the input in our lives. With the click of a mouse, we can order anything we want, from a bicycle to cleaning supplies. We don't even have to leave the house. But then, as we accumulate more and more "stuff," we need to find more places to store all that stuff. It's a never-ending cycle. You can see how emotionally and mentally exhausting all this is for you and your family.

In order to be mentally free of clutter, we must get rid of the physical things that are cluttering our lives. It is crucial to get rid of the junk that's stopping you from pursuing your life's core value and purpose. Release the stress of the past as you release your hold on all the trinkets and gadgets you've been needlessly keeping over the years. Forgive people who have wronged you as you forgive yourself for letting junk pile up in your house, and move on. That's easier said than done, but it will help you improve your overall mental state and contribute to your overall happiness.

Clarify your life priorities

Many of us suffer from procrastination. While this is a fairly common human behavior, it's also frequently a cause of significant stress in our lives. The more we put off doing things that need to be done, the more stressed we become. But the thing is, we're always putting things we don't want to do on the back burner because we imagine they'll be too difficult or time-consuming to complete, and then we end up not getting them done at all or having to do them hastily with poor quality.

Unfortunately, this seems to be a modern problem that is not easily fixed. Think about it: Let's say an employee trying to finish a certain project by the deadline but has been putting it off over the past few days. The deadline approaches, and he realizes he cannot complete the work on time because he's been procrastinating for so long. He asks for an extension and is unable to receive it, leading him to rush to throw together the project, with lackluster results.

This is a fairly typical scenario for the average employee. We are always chasing deadlines, even though we are fully capable of managing our time. You simply need to have a to-do list and stick to it. Prioritizing the items on your to-do list is the most fundamental thing you can do to avoid procrastination.

There are six main areas of your life in which you should establish your priorities and determine how you want to spend your time while having clarity in your life.

1. Spiritual/personal growth

The Bible says in 2 Chronicles 32:8, "With him is only the arm of flesh, but with us is the LORD our God to help us and to fight our battles" (NKJV).

Without God, we can do nothing. But with God, we can do everything. One of the best antidotes to low self-esteem and low self-confidence is faith in God. Yes, one of the most powerful things you can have in life is faith in God. Faith is what empowers you to feel that you can do anything.

Whatever plans you have, always remember God is still the one who decides what's best for you. So, surrender your plans to God. Proverbs 20:24 tells us, "The LORD directs a man's steps." You plan, but let God direct your steps.

Start your day by reading the Bible, even if only for 5 to 10 minutes each day. Talk to God first before anything else; release your worries to Him. Pray for good health, protection, love, joy, peace, happiness, enthusiasm, and abundance for you and your family.

Do this every single day, and you will discover the secret to gaining confidence and self-esteem: faith in God. In addition to listening to God's Spirit, you must also listen to your heart.

Psalm 37:4-5 (NKJV) states: "Delight yourself also in the LORD, and He shall give you the desires of your heart. Commit your way to the LORD, trust also in Him, and he shall bring it to pass."

God gives us the desires of our heart for a reason. We all have different hopes. My hopes may differ from yours, and your wishes may be different from mine.

If you want to know God's will for your life, listen to what your heart is telling you. God created our hearts to discern things that He wants us to do or not to do. Your heart gives you signals, or warnings, about whether what you're about to do is in God's plan for you or not.

2. Marriage and family

Many studies prove that the number one predictor of happiness is the quality of your social relationships, both at home with your loved ones and at work. Science has shown that bonds with others make us happier and more productive, committed, energetic, and resilient. When we have a network of people we can count on, we recover faster from setbacks.

Thanks to relationships, we achieve more, and we have a greater sense of purpose. Relationships are a necessity. No one can survive or prosper without connections, and they make a real difference in mental health. Being happy and sharing this happiness with others will improve your relationships.

Similarly, when you go through hardships and difficulties, your social support system will help you overcome them. Indeed, the most important relationships are those with your nearest and dearest. Family is not only important—it's everything!

3. Health and fitness

Go for a run or a walk in the morning hours, and it will energize you for the whole day. Take the time to walk through the woods or on the beach to disconnect from the fast and stressful rhythm of the lives we lead. Watch a sunset or a sunrise. Listening to the silence and peace will help you to relax. Taking a walk will re-energize your body, mind, and soul.

A Stanford study concluded that walking improves creative thinking (Wong, 2014), and that walking for just half an hour a day, every day, is just as good as exercising in terms of the health benefits. Walking 30 minutes a day will decrease cholesterol, improve performance, lower stress levels, improve immune system, eliminate fat, and boost mood. It might even shield you against burnout. Even better, you can analyze your emotions while you're walking (just as long as you don't start overthinking them, of course!). Finally, taking a daily walk will allow you to fall asleep more comfortably and have a better and more refreshing sleep at night.

So when are you going to start walking for half an hour every day? Try it for just 30 days and see how this makes you feel! In fact, after only a week, you might see significant improvements in your health and mood.

The benefits of exercising at least every other day are countless:

- Increased self-esteem

- Less stress and anxiety

- Better mood and higher energy

- Enhanced work performance

- Improved sleep quality

- Weight loss

- Less risk of physical diseases

The likelihood of diabetes, osteoporosis, heart failure, high cholesterol, and even particular forms of cancer reduces significantly through exercise. After a run, your brain is more open to creating new neural pathways. Your memory improves, meaning that you retain the material you have learned much better, and you become much more creative.

4. Life management and self-improvement

The best thing you can do to decrease mental clutter and enhance your personal and professional growth is to invest in yourself. Make a firm commitment to becoming the best person you can be. Invest some of your earnings in books, training, or other personal development tools.

Keep an open mind and a desire to learn new things and improve yourself.

One possible effect of investing in your personal development is that you may become more beneficial to your organization due to your increased knowledge. There are numerous options available, including in-person and online trainings, that will enable you to enhance a number of different skills. You can learn effective strategies or tools that will transform your life in a two- or four-hour workshop style class. You can also decide to go all-in and hire a life coach to help you work on yourself.

However, feel free to start with easier and less expensive methods, like reading a book, listening to an audiobook, or taking an online course. Some people make it a habit to read at least one book per week, take a new class every two months, and/or enroll in at least one seminar or training course per year.

Be careful, though. Don't fall into the trap of thinking that you always need to take just one more course or read just one more book before starting your dream project. It is imperative that you apply what you learn as soon as possible after receiving training or education. Many people take one class after another and never stop to assess or implemented what they've learned. It's as if they're waiting until they become perfect at a particular skill before they'll attempt to use their knowledge. My friend, this is a colossal mistake and is called sabotaging yourself.

5. Leisure/social

Are you unsure whether you should declutter? There are a few signals you can use to assess whether your social life is in need of decluttering. Consider the following to determine which of the three warning indicators you should be on the lookout for:

1. Mindless scrolling

What percentage of your time do you spend looking through your social media feeds and scrolling mindlessly through post after post? While we may be unaware of it, technology is increasingly encroaching on our lives and our mental health. We require technology to facilitate our life, but we should not allow it to devour too much of our precious time.

2. Online 24/7

Do you log out of your social media accounts after you've used them? Nowadays, no one ever logs out; they're online 24 hours a day, and our phones are constantly updating us about new posts, comments, likes, and chats. The thing is, when our social networking apps are in standby mode like this, we're more inclined to check in on our gadgets mindlessly every minute or so (literally).

3. Immediately clicking on notifications

How frequently do you immediately check out a new post/instant message upon receiving a notification? It may be faster to count the number of times we have disregarded an alert instead. Most of the notifications we click instantly cannot be regarded as remotely necessary, and doing so may even be detrimental to your mental health.

If you find yourself engaging in these behaviors, your online habits may have gotten out of control. It might be time to reassess your use of social media and the internet and declutter by evaluating your online connections, notification settings, and privacy settings to give yourself more of a break.

Mindful Goal Setting

Mindful goal setting entails creating timely, measurable, and specific goals. If you are determined to achieve something in your life, then I'm sure you understand what goal setting is and how it works.

We've all tried to set goals for ourselves one way or another. We end every year with New Year's Resolutions. Some goals last a few months, and some don't even survive January. We're so used to failing to reach the goals that, at some point, we give up on setting them. After all, they don't work, right? At the beginning of every year, we get excited about change; we decide we'll "lose X pounds of fat this year and build Y pounds of muscle" or "make Z amount of money." But we don't, and it's depressing.

I'll let you in on a small secret to setting goals that do work, and that's what we've been building up to in this book. Most of the goals we choose are based on physical or performance-related achievements. We want to look a certain way, save a certain amount of money, or perform so well at our jobs that we'll inevitably get a promotion. While those are the results we want, we're approaching the goal-setting process from completely the wrong direction.

We often look at goals simply as paths to the rewards we'll get from them, but we give very little thought to who we'll become by achieving these goals. It's important to recognize that the results of a goal that goes against our nature or identity won't stick around for too long. So, instead of the goal of losing X pounds a month, why not set a goal of becoming a fit person with a healthy lifestyle? Instead of wanting to make X amount of money, how about deciding to become the type of person who can make X amount of money?

Setting a goal that focuses on the journey instead of the end result makes all the difference in the world. The wrong approach will make each step a struggle until you either give up on the goal (because it's going against your nature) or use up every ounce of willpower on this goal, discarding everything else in your life. The right approach focuses on who you'll become due to this goal. It builds a constructive framework of habits to paint the bigger picture, so you can grow in every aspect of your being, one step at a time. It is possible to be content in the present while still planning for the future. The idea is to savor every moment while mindfully planning your future and appreciating each step along the way.

Essentially, you need to discover what gets you up in the morning. What keeps you going? What drives you? You should deeply consider what you want to do with your life, how you want to live, and your unique goals and aspirations. Don't let anyone get in the way of your journey, and don't hold back when it comes to doing whatever it takes to become the best version of yourself.

To set identity-based goals, choose an identity you want to achieve. The choice of a new identity can be based on several things. You can decide where you want to go and become the kind of person who'd be able to go there, or you can focus on where you're stuck in life and set out to change the current version of yourself. However, what works best is to build your new identity based on your vision of who you want to be and your desire to stop feeling stuck.

Then you need to prove to yourself that you can, indeed, become this person. Identify the habits or behaviors that are preventing you from becoming that person, and form new habits that will help you develop the desired identity. All it takes is one small win in the direction of the goal for you to start believing you can achieve it. Make this identity the central point for building your framework of habits, which will all integrate into your lifestyle. By taking these steps slowly but surely, you'll instill belief and rewire the habits in your brain in the most effective way possible.

Before you know it, you'll have developed all the habits you desired, and overcome the ones that were keeping you stuck. You'll experience your new identity, enjoying the new life you've created for yourself.

In the process of achieving your new identity, there are a few things you can do to make the journey a little smoother. We'll discuss them below.

Create quarterly SMART goals

It's best practice to break down your overarching goals into smaller ones and prioritize the goals you want to accomplish on a daily, weekly, or monthly basis. Apply the SMART formula to each of your goals. SMART provides a good guideline for achieving your dreams. The acronym SMART stands for:

- **Specific:** Does your goal include who, what, where, when, and why?

- **Measurable:** Does your goal use accurate timeframes, numbers, or other units of measurement?

- **Attainable:** Does your goal push the boundaries of what you think you can do without being outside the realm of possibility?

- **Relevant:** Is your goal in line with your true desires?

- **Time-bound:** Does your goal have definite deadlines?

Aligning your goals with the SMART framework and setting quarterly (rather than yearly) timelines to achieve them makes it easier for you to do everything you set out to do.

Here's how to make your SMART ideas a reality:

1. Determine what is most important to you; concentrate on three to four areas of your life maximum to avoid becoming overwhelmed.

2. Focus on three-month goals. Life is in continual flux, and long-term goals can be too vague and

discouraging, which is why people often give up on their New Year's resolutions.

3. Create a schedule using a weekly review. Make a weekly action plan that considers your duties, priorities, and available time.

4. Take action on your goals. Convert each goal into a project by working backward from your target deadline. Schedule opportunities to work on your goals, and convert them into deliverables by working on your key objectives first thing in the morning (or whenever you feel most energized). Schedule time for individual actions by grouping them together.

5. Review your goals daily to keep them fresh in your memory.

6. Examine your quarterly objectives. Ask yourself, "Have I gotten the desired result? Which strategies were successful and which were not? Am I devoting 100 percent of my effort to achieving these objectives?"

Identify what's important to you

Below are a few tips to help you focus on the important things in your life to help you achieve your goals.

- Everything you experience is based on your mind; train it on a daily basis!

- Detachment from intrusive thoughts and emotions can be achieved through focused breathing and meditation.

- Take control of your thoughts by interrupting, rephrasing, and challenging them in order to reduce their power over you.

- Make goals centered on your core principles to help you take focused action and maintain your self-esteem.

- Be present and conscious in your relationships to avoid many of the tensions and emotional pain that come with human interaction.

- Keep your home and digital life organized to avoid being distracted from your values, priorities, and ambitions.

Create an environment of clarity

Do you look forward to your weekends because you're always dying to get out of the office? Are you bored with your job? Do you dread gloomy Mondays? Your answers to these questions will help you get on the right track to finding meaningful work for your life, contributing to your happiness and fulfillment.

As you think about your motivation, consider what will make you happy in the long run. What talent or special skills do you possess that will be helpful in a particular job? What interests do you have that can benefit you in your desired position? Think about the things that light you on fire and help you contribute to others and their development, and you will experience mental clarity and a better life.

God wants to bless you. The blessing of Jacob is also for you. Reclaim it today:

"By the God of your father who will help you, And by the Almighty who will bless you With blessings of heaven above, Blessings of the deep that lies beneath, Blessings of the breasts and of the womb."

– Genesis 49:25 (NKJV)

No matter what the situation you are going through, this promise is for you in Christ. God wants to give you His blessings. In God's Word, we read:

"He remembers his covenant forever, the promise he made, for a thousand generations"

– 1 Chronicles 16:15 (NIV)

As Paul said in Galatians 4:28, "Now we, brethren, as Isaac was, are children of promise." That means you can claim all the promises of the heirs of Abraham. With God's promises, you will have the power to pass through stormy days. It's time to have a balanced life and stand on the promises of our Heavenly Father.

Key Takeaways

- Mental clutter can be caused by stress and anxiety, but it can also be impacted by a cluttered physical environment.

- To reduce mental clutter, clean up your physical space as well as your digital space. Consider logging out of social media and allowing your mind time to find clarity away from the busyness of daily life.

- Defining your core priorities and values will help you find balance because you'll be able to focus on what's truly important to you.

- Setting SMART (specific, measurable, attainable, relevant, and time-bound) goals each quarter will keep you on track to attaining the balanced, fulfilled life you desire.

- Remember that God wants to bless you, and if you rely on Him, you will find it easier to achieve a harmonious and peaceful life.

Time to Take Action

It is essential to realize that the journey to becoming a more positive and balanced person is a process. It will not look the same for everyone. Some people require more time to process and get over past situations, and others need help in decluttering their physical and mental environment; however, once you're able to move past these challenges, you'll find you can focus on becoming more positive.

Don't be discouraged if nothing changes for a little while even after you start implementing the tips in this chapter. It takes practice. If you're used to always being negative and dwelling on pessimistic, anxiety-driven thoughts in your head, it will take a little while for you to transform that into positivity and mental clarity. Be patient with yourself. Recognize that things can change, but it takes time.

Life is short. We have to take advantage of every opportunity to find joy and meaning in life because that's what is most important. Life isn't about having a fancy job, making a lot of money, or accumulating a lot of stuff. Rather, it's about appreciating the simple everyday treasures life offers and finding a deeper purpose.

This requires having a thankful heart that is willing to take in every moment and savor the goodness of it while finding time to say "thank you" to God for the blessings you have. Once you do that, you'll experience freedom and joy like never before. It will free you from all your anxieties and stress and lead you to a more delightful and prosperous future. You'll experience a fantastic transformation in your life.

A balanced life will help you overcome overthinking and cultivate a new attitude. The next chapter dives into the psychology of stress and managing the anger that often comes with stress. Then we will discuss dialectical behavior therapy, endurance, and steps towards success.

CHAPTER SEVEN

Overcome Overthinking by Cultivating New Attitudes

"Can any one of you by worrying add a single hour to your life?"

– Matthew 6:27 (NIV)

Lesson from the vision of Lu Xun: Face your reality

On September 25, 1881, in Shaoxing, China, Lu Xun was born. After some misfortunes, he left his town in 1898 to study at the Jiangnan Naval Academy. Four years later, after graduating with the third-highest scores of his class, he received a Chinese government scholarship to get a Western-style education in Japan. He went there to study medicine.

During Lu Xun's life, China was at its darkest and most helpless time. The Japanese had defeated the country in 1894. Japan's ambition was to be the leader of East Asia. Thus, Lu Xun was humiliated and frustrated by his identity as a Chinese citizen living in Japan. One day during his medical studies, he was shocked by a slideshow in which some Japanese executed a Chinese man. This event pushed him to radically challenge the situation of his country. Instead of becoming a doctor, he became a writer in order to help his country face reality and pursue change.

In 1909, he returned to China to become a writer, essayist, poet, and literary critic. He is among the most talented writers of 20th-century Chinese literature. Lu Xun's top priority was to rejuvenate his fellow Chinese by asking them to face China's harsh reality and explore change through his writings. Today, China has surpassed Japan and is the second-largest economy in the world.

The story of Lu Xun brings out the concept of facing reality and overcoming challenges. In times of crisis, many people are tempted to flee from scenarios that could get them into trouble or put them in an unfortunate situation. However, it is not always possible to prevent a problem from happening. Sometimes you have to face those problems head-on. It is, therefore, best to figure out ways that you can respond to the things that are stressing you out.

The next time you're in this type of situation, remember the story of Lu Xun. Persevere, and do not worry. There is hope. Your challenge may be overwhelming, but do not overthink it, and do not stay in despair. Face the reality and remember that there is always hope. Talk to God when you're at your lowest points. He will always make a way.

The Psychology of Stress

Stress is a powerful force in our everyday lives. It's impossible to pretend that it doesn't exist. It is natural to have periods of stress, but too much can be harmful to your health and affect your happiness, relationships, and overall quality of life. Stress impacts so many aspects of our lives that understanding its psychology may help us keep it at bay in the future. If you can identify the sources of stress in your life and how they impact you, it will help you to reduce your stress. The best way you can deal with stress is to prepare yourself for it.

Facing the stress

The first step to avoiding stress is going through it in the first place. If you cannot anticipate the sources of stress in your life, you will have no way of dealing with them effectively.

When faced with hardship and possible loss, we often hold back on what we're passionate about. For example, you may take a job that isn't exactly fulfilling because you're stressed about not having enough money to support your family. However, sometimes facing the stress and going through that difficult situation is necessary for growth.

To experience profound change within yourself, it's essential that you face up to the things that may negatively impact you. Pay attention to the sources of stress in your life and then find ways to solve those problems.

One thing that makes us so unique as humans is our ability to take a negative experience and turn it into a positive one. In order to do this effectively, you must face your problems head-on.

Coping with stressful times

To master stress, you must first learn to relax in stressful situations. We often find ourselves experiencing stress because of our reactions to the things that happen to us. It is essential to understand why you are stressed and what you can do about it. Once you've taken control of your reactions, you'll find the situation is less likely to cause emotional distress. Facing the source of stress before it begins will prepare you for dealing with the stresses that come your way later on.

Anger and Stress Management

Anger is a normal, active emotion, neither good nor bad. It conveys a message like any other emotion, telling you that a situation is perturbing, unjust, or threatening. However, if your reaction to anger is to explode, that message never has an opportunity to be passed on. So, while feeling angry when you've been wronged or when you're stressed is perfectly normal, anger becomes an issue when you're expressing it in a way that harms yourself or others.

You may feel that expressing your anger is beneficial, that those around you are overly sensitive, and your anger is justifiable, or that you need to exhibit your rage to gain respect. But the real issue is that anger is much more likely to affect how other people see you, impair your judgment, and hamper success.

Controlling your anger

Anger can be a helpful tool, or it can be hideously destructive. It's like a fire. Some situations require an immediate response fueled by righteous anger, such as witnessing some type of abuse or bullying, whether physical or psychological. But in other cases, small things might cause your anger to build to the point where you risk losing control over your emotions unjustifiably.

If you feel that this is happening to you, try the following strategies:

1. **Walk away.** If you're in the middle of an extremely uncomfortable or stressful situation that sparks anger, it's hard not to say the first thing that comes to mind, but you may regret it later. Thus, it may be best to remove yourself from the situation.

2. **Use deep breathing.** Deep breathing has been found to be one of the quickest ways to reduce the intensity of your anger (Thomas & Aiken, 2019).

3. **Practice relaxation.** Immerse yourself in something you enjoy. Look for something to engage in that will divert your attention and help

you to calm down once you take a break from the situation. Try reading, listening to music, or any other relaxing activity.

4. **Exercise.** Non-strenuous exercise is a good option. Take a walk, ride your bike, or stretch your muscles. This might help you relax by releasing tension in your muscles.

Dialectical Behavior Therapy

Dialectical behavior therapy (DBT) teaches techniques for managing uncomfortable emotions like stress and anger and reducing relationship conflict. DBT consists of four main areas:

1. *Mindfulness*, which aims to improve a person's ability to admit fault and be aware of the reality of the present situation;

2. *Distress tolerance*, which aims to increase a person's endurance rather than letting them avoid the negativity of the situation;

3. *Self-control*, which refers to methods for coping with and changing strong emotions that are producing challenges in one's life; and

4. *Interpersonal effectiveness*, which refers to the skills that enable a person to engage with others confidently, have self-respect, and build relationships.

Our emotions influence our goals and behavior. The brain internalizes these messages from our emotions—perhaps we think we need to be successful, we need to be perfect, we need to be rich, and so on, and that anything outside this equation is a failure. Anything other than perfection is a threat. When we do not achieve these high standards, it creates more stress and anger. We cannot expect our brains to differentiate between real-life threats and imagined ones. Worrying about an event taking place in the future could trigger the same threat response as a very real tornado coming at you in the moment. Because of the brain's physiology, these negative emotions are thus triggered many times throughout the day if we dwell on stressful thoughts.

DBT's Core Actionable Skills

Let's dive into the four critical skills of DBT as defined in the previous section: mindfulness, distress tolerance, mood management, and interpersonal effectiveness.

Mindfulness

Mindfulness is defined as being aware of and focused on the current moment rather than the past or the future (Brown & Ryan, 2003). The following are some DBT skills for practicing mindfulness:

- Concentrate on the present moment.

- Without passing judgment, observe your thoughts, emotions, and bodily sensations.

- Engage in mindful breathing to bring yourself into the present moment.

- During attentive meditation, be friendly and sympathetic to yourself.

Distress tolerance

When people are overwhelmed by emotions, they often try to deal with them to feel better in the moment. Unfortunately, this can include using substances to numb the pain or engaging in some form of self-destructive behavior. However, these tactics create even more emotional distress in the long run. Learning to better manage those overpowering feelings is what distress tolerance is all about.

The following DBT skills can help you enhance your distress tolerance:

- Divert your attention away from undesirable ideas and feelings.

- Accept what you can't change and focus on what you can change (referred to as "radical acceptance").

- Utilize self-soothing techniques, such as paying attention to your five senses to relax and soothe yourself.

- Visualize a safe, serene location, such as the beach or the mountains.

- Use your spirituality to empower yourself.

Emotional control

When an individual has a history of trauma or feels threatened or abandoned, they may experience emotional extremes that they cannot control. Emotional dysregulation is the term for this. The person may become excessively reactive and self-destructive when triggered or emotionally overwhelmed. Brain researchers have discovered that patients with emotional dysregulation may have abnormalities in the neurocircuitry in the brain that governs emotion. However, these abnormalities can be dealt with using some coping skills to help with emotional regulation.

The following are some DBT emotion management skills:

- Recognize and name the feelings you're experiencing.

- Recognize how your emotions are influenced by your beliefs and behavior.

- Acknowledge and address self-destructive behavior.

- Boost pleasant feelings.

- Manage strong feelings.

Emotions are chemical and physical signals that communicate your feelings and what's going on in your body. Extreme reactive emotions are helpful when confronted with an immediate threat or danger, but they are less useful in relationships and at work. DBT was created to assist people who are experiencing strong emotions in learning how to manage them and better their lives.

Interpersonal effectiveness

Interpersonal effectiveness techniques are all about increasing one's social skills. Setting limits and controlling disagreements while respecting others is necessary for managing emotions and emotional reactivity in partnerships.

Among the interpersonal effectiveness skills taught in DBT are:

- Paying close attention to people so you can comprehend what they're thinking and experiencing
- Making straightforward requests for what you want while maintaining your relationships
- Listening actively rather than passively

Life Skills for Endurance and Resilience

"'So do not fear; I will provide for you and your little ones.'
Thus he comforted them and spoke kindly to them."

– Genesis 50:21 (NKJV)

Surround yourself with success

The entrepreneur and motivational speaker Jim Rohn once said, "You are the average of the five people you spend the most time with." Reread that sentence.

What kind of crowd do you run with? What kind of audience do you have? You will become more and more like the people you associate with. Do you spend your time with winners or with people who make excuses? Do you spend your time with people who blame others or people who take responsibility for their actions? Do you spend time with cowards who flee from their fears or people who bravely face their challenges?

Suppose you're hanging out with the correct people. You'll embrace their way of thinking and habits. You'll begin to focus on your goals daily, and anything you think about regularly will manifest in your life. Are you aware of this? It's time to take a look at your entourage.

People who are sincerely committed to conquering fear and realizing their goals surround themselves with people who share their thinking or are on the same level as them (or a higher one). These are people who will inspire you and drive you to reach your objectives. To be free of fear, you must raise the bar and your standards while allowing others to hold you accountable, which means running among winners.

Adopt a growth mindset

When scared, we have a tendency to isolate ourselves. What happens if you make a blunder? What if you fail? Maybe you begin to believe that you can't grow and improve at all, that you're not capable of doing so. That is the fear that is preventing you from moving forward.

Adopting a growth mindset is one of the most effective ways to overcome fear and anxiety. It's not about reaching your objectives immediately and being flawless at all times. Stop striving for perfection. Be at ease with what you don't know, and push on regardless. A growth mindset is built on this foundation.

As you attempt to overcome your fear of failure, you'll notice there are many ups and downs along the route. You'll be one step closer to achieving your objectives if you realize that the road to success entails growth and change. Always remember that mistakes are part of life, and adopt the mindset of learning from criticism and feedback.

Find valuable insight in pain

No one enjoys being in agony or feeling stressed and angry all the time. The majority of people go to considerable lengths to avoid it. Pain, however, is a powerful teacher. Painful experiences become excellent opportunities for growth if you understand that your life and sometimes efforts to achieve your goals will be painful. When you stop seeing pain (or stress) as a danger to your life, it loses its potency and becomes a new instrument for dealing with fear and obstacles.

Everyone faces difficulties from time to time, whether the setbacks are personal or professional. What is important is what you learn from your experiences and how you apply those lessons in the future. Rather than allowing sorrow and fear to govern the game and your actions, actively learn from those terrible experiences to take charge of your own life.

Decide right now that you're going to run your life, not the other way around. Consider that pain is a profound teacher. Rather than allowing sorrow and fear to influence your actions, deliberately choose to learn from those difficult experiences so that you may take charge of your life. Reframe your fear and give it a new meaning so that it becomes your ally and guides you to progress to the next level.

Visualize your goals

You've already done the mental work of discovering the genuine reasons you're limiting yourself and defining your life's "must-haves." However, overcoming fear takes daily practice of these habits to result in real change. Recognize your problems, but devote your strength and efforts to finding answers.

One of these solutions is goal visualization. It is used by some of the world's most prominent athletes, entertainers, and businesspeople.

Visualizing your goal establishes your concentration and focus. Visualize yourself succeeding and fully commit to your goal. You can also meditate on achieving your goal. You'll begin to train your brain to believe that anything is possible—a necessary step toward conquering fear.

How to Manage Your Time and Energy to Move Forward

Every day, we face a barrage of deadlines, tasks, and appointments. We're just busy living our lives. We have less time and energy to spend on ourselves. This leads to stress, confusion, and exhaustion. However, if we can learn how to work smarter and not more complicated, we can lead a more fulfilling life with the time we do have.

You've probably heard the cliché that we need to spend our time doing what we love, but maybe you often find yourself with little relief from the tedious tasks that make up most of your day-to-day life. Managing your time and energy in this situation is vital in order to develop efficient ways to get things done with minimum effort.

The three D's

There are different methods you can use to prepare for the future or plan your schedule, but first, take inventory of how you currently manage your time based on the three D's: days, distractions, and decisions. These three D's are essential for managing your time.

Days: First, calculate how many hours per week are available to you. Include any extra time that could potentially be added to your schedule.

Distractions: Consider who or what might distract you from achieving your goals. Then find ways to minimize their interference. For example, if your significant other always complains about you not spending time with them, it might be a good idea to schedule some time in the evenings to focus on your relationship.

Decisions: A big part of time management is making a realistic yet efficient schedule. Make a list of the top priorities you want to accomplish for the week. Put the tasks in order of importance, with the most important first. This is a significant step in time management because it helps you determine if the things on your list are really what you want to accomplish or if they are time-wasters. You may have a lot of things going on at work but decide that prioritizing the pursuit of a hobby or personal interest a few hours per week will make you much happier.

Find happiness

Are you ready to say yes to happy choices? Deciding to have more happiness in your life is a serious matter. After all, your happiness affects your whole life: your self-esteem, relationships, physical and mental health, and maybe even the amount of time you have left to live.

Yes—it's really that important.

Don't let stress get the best of you. Life is tough. You will need strength and courage in difficult times. God knows that. After the death of Moses, Joshua had to lead the people of Israel and fight many kings. This task was monumental. God said to Joshua:

"Be strong and courageous because you will lead these people to inherit the land, I swore to their ancestors to give them. Be strong and very courageous. Be careful to obey all the law my servant Moses gave you; do not turn from it to the right or the left, that you may be successful wherever you go. Keep this Book of the Law always on your lips; meditate on it day and night so that you may be careful to do everything written in it. Then you will be prosperous and successful. Have I not commanded you? Be strong and courageous. Do not be afraid; do not be discouraged, for the Lord your God will be with you wherever you go."

– Joshua 1:6-9 (NKJV)

God commands Joshua to "Be strong and very courageous" three times (verses 6, 7, 9). But in verse 9, God said this is not just advice; it's a command ("Have I not commanded you?").

We read in Joshua 12:24 that Joshua defeated 31 kings. That means 31 dangerous fights—31 periods of high stress. But it's also 31 times that God showed His power against the enemy, 31 times that God kept His promises, and 31 times that God saved His people.

Today, you may be fighting many battles: Fighting to succeed in life, fighting against a disease, fighting in your workplace, fighting within your family, fighting against anxiety or depression. But do not worry; if God gave Joshua victory over 31 battles, no matter how many battles you have, know that God can give you victory also. God will be with you in each of your fights. He has never failed anyone. The fight may be intense, but victory is guaranteed with Him.

Do not overthink your battles. Instead, cultivate a new attitude. Believe in God. Trust Him. God will fight for you.

Key Takeaways

- Don't waste time overthinking your life's problems, but instead develop a new mindset. Face your problems head-on and look for solutions.

- Learn to control your anger, because in the long term, anger as a reaction to stress is harmful to your physical and mental health.

- When you're living in the moment, it's much harder to dwell on the past or be concerned about the future. Mindfulness will assist you in becoming more aware of the present moment.

- Paying attention to your thoughts can assist you in being more conscious of your negative mental patterns. You can educate your brain to think differently with practice. Building healthier behaviors over time can assist you in developing the mental muscle you require to become less stressed and create a new mindset.

- Always have faith in God. He will grant you victory.

Time to Take Action

Sometimes the best way to overcome feelings of unworthiness, anger, or stress is to ride them out, especially if you feel as if you're out of viable options or have too much to deal with.

Keep fighting on—get dressed and do what you have to do, with the view that something positive might present itself to you. Life has a way of knocking even the best of us down, but that very same life also frequently surprises us with new ways of looking at things, better ways of solving our problems, and opportunities to get over what was seemingly an impossibly large obstacle.

You've made it this far and have learned many strategies for managing your tendency to overthink, anxiety, and stress. The last chapter will look at steps to help you master your emotions and live a purposeful life.

CHAPTER EIGHT

Steps To Master Your Emotions
and Live a Life of Purpose

"Set your mind on things above, not on things on the earth."

– Colossians 3:2 (NKJV)

Sky's emotional rollercoaster

Let's look at an example of recognizing moments when something triggers our emotions, which is the first step to mastering them:

Sky was in her room doing homework when her mother walked in and asked if she had finished all her chores for the day. She quickly replied that she hadn't, which was why she was doing homework. When her mother left, Sky was left with an odd feeling. She was almost angry, and she wasn't sure why.

Later that same day, when Sky was in the kitchen making a grilled cheese sandwich, her father walked in and asked her if she needed help. A little annoyed, she replied that it was okay, that she was doing it herself and didn't need any help. Once again, she felt almost angry, and she wasn't sure where those feelings were coming from. She didn't think much of it, blaming it on being tired, and continued with her day.

At dinner time, when the family was gathered at the table, Sky's brother looked at her with a frown and asked if she was okay. Perplexed, Sky asked why he was asking that. Her brother replied that she looked angry or something, which made Sky even more furious. She left the table feeling annoyed and puzzled. She wasn't sure where any of these feelings were coming from, but she was growing incredibly frustrated.

Sitting on her bed and trying to read a book, she realized something must have triggered her. She wasn't sure what it was, but something about the interactions she'd had must have annoyed her for some reason.

Sky lay in bed that night and thought about the possibilities of what could have triggered her. After that day, every time she had an interaction that generated a feeling she wasn't expecting, she tried to get to the root of it, asking herself: *Why does this bother me? Why am I feeling like this?*

All of us occasionally feel like Sky did in this story. We get upset, frustrated, or angry and we don't understand why, but we realize that it must have something to do with our interactions with others throughout the day. When that happens, it's time to sit down and reflect on *why* you feel the way you do.

What Is an Emotion?

For many years, psychologists and philosophers have engaged in spirited debate on the nature of emotions.

Generally speaking, emotions result from interacting with others in a specific setting and culture. Various theories in neuroscience explain how a human being's brain can generate emotions by combining bodily perceptions and cognitive appraisals. Suppose something shocking happens to you today; it is natural and very normal to develop emotions such as sadness or anger.

Today, there are two main scientific approaches that can be employed to explain what emotions are: cognitive appraisal theory and James–Lange theory.

Cognitive appraisal theory says that emotions are judgments on how the situation you are in currently meets the goals you have set. According to this theory, positive emotions such as happiness express goals being fulfilled (Nelson-Coffey, 2022). On the other hand, sadness and negative emotions depict unfulfilled goals and disappointments in life and be a form of anger towards a stumbling block to your goals.

The James–Lange theory of emotion, developed by psychologists William James and Carl Lange, argues that emotions are just perceptions of various changes in your body in different situations, and thus emotions arise as a result of a certain physiological state.

These two theories can be integrated to develop a unified definition of emotions. We can, therefore, describe emotions as one's mental state, associated with the nervous system and linked to the chemical changes that take place in the body. These chemical changes are usually linked to feelings, thoughts, and behavioral responses. Emotions can also be termed negative or positive experiences linked to certain patterns of physiological functions in the body. The bottom line is that emotions are part of our reaction to the cognitive, behavioral, and physiological changes we undergo.

What Is Emotional Mastery?

Emotional mastery is the act of becoming aware of and learning to control one's emotional states (how one feels at a given instant) and utilizing them to one's benefit.

The emotional mastery process begins with identifying and understanding your feelings. Once you have assessed what you're feeling, reflect on what triggered the emotions and identify the thoughts that continue to add fuel to your unhappiness.

If these thoughts can't be resolved, you need to seek out healthier ways of responding to situations so that you can feel better about yourself and your life.

Let Go of Your Negative Emotions

If you have a negative thought process in your mind today, it isn't baseless. It has its roots in the very same survival instinct that enabled our ancestors to survive in the most dangerous situations. However, there is a line beyond which even helpful things can become toxic. If you let your brain run wild without any control, it will keep playing out fear-inducing scenarios, preventing you from taking action. Your mind knows that the safest bet for survival is to remain in your shell. The outside world is unpredictable, and there are forces beyond our control. However, becoming a slave to this mentality is also dangerous.

Negative thought patterns arise in your mind as a natural response to certain situations. The extent of the negative thoughts depends on your perception of the threat. Most of the time, there is really no threat at all; you're simply scared to take action, and your mind starts showing you the worst possible outcomes. This leads to inaction, procrastination, fear, and anxiety. If you fall into this trap, you are destined to fail. Inaction will get you nowhere. If you want to move forward in your life to grow, change, and improve, you need to act.

Excessive negative thought patterns are a part of mind clutter. Your mind is filled with too much negativity, and this is reflected in negative thinking. This can be a dangerous thing if it goes unchecked. It can make you indecisive, frightened, and weak, afraid to take a chance on something new. <u>Your</u> risk-taking ability will falter, and you'll become too fearful to make any decisions at all. This is a terrible state to be in the first place. You'll lose control over your life, and instead, your anxiety will begin deciding how you live your life. This will take a toll on your personal and professional life, health, family, relationships, career, and more.

Transform Negative Emotions into Positive Ones

It is essential to replace negativity with positivity; however, that's not as easy as it sounds. Most people misunderstand the whole idea of negative thinking. Happiness does not necessarily depend on the presence or absence of negative thoughts, but rather, on how we handle these negative thoughts.

Despite the setbacks and obstacles you face, it is essential to try to maintain a sense of optimism. The benefits of avoiding negative thinking are more significant than most people think. In fact, research suggests that positive thinkers enjoy life more than pessimists do (De Meza & Dawson, 2020). When it comes to physiological and psychological health, as well as stress levels, optimistic people are way ahead of the game. Thinking positively is an excellent way to heal, but first you need to stop listening to your mind's anxiety-driven falsehoods.

It's also helpful to try to figure out the origin of your negative thoughts. Remember, negative thoughts stem from wrong assumptions and beliefs; therefore, merely ignoring them is not good enough. You need to challenge those thoughts and replace them with positive ones. Everyone is worthy of love and happiness, and that includes you—don't forget this.

Control Your Emotions

Emotions are the most pervasive, compelling, and potentially unpleasant force in our existence. Our emotions guide us daily to take risks because we're enthused about fresh possibilities. We weep because we've been wronged, and we make sacrifices out of love. Our emotions, without a doubt, have great control over our reasoning minds in dictating our thoughts, intentions, and actions. However, when we react to our emotions too quickly or with the wrong feelings, we frequently behave in ways that we subsequently regret.

You might find that your emotions swing dangerously from one extreme to the other. Maybe you're on the verge of fury over a small argument with your spouse, but then in bliss thanks to your favorite TV show or a hug from your child. Like many other aspects of life, emotions benefit from moderation and a reasonable perspective.

This doesn't mean it's a bad thing to fall head over heels in love or excitedly jump for joy when receiving good news. These are wonderful, joyous parts of human life. On the other hand, however, you must treat negative emotions with utmost caution.

Negative emotions such as fury, envy, and resentment tend to spin out of control easily, especially when provoked. These emotions can spread like weeds over time, training the mind to function on negative emotions and taking control of your daily life. Have you ever met someone who is always angry or hostile? They weren't born with that personality. They simply allowed certain emotions to simmer within them so long that they became inbred sentiments that arise far too frequently.

So, how can we avoid functioning on the wrong types of emotion and master our emotions even in the most trying of situations?

In our darkest moments, faith in God is our saving grace. Pray and ask God to reveal the best path forward when you're overcome with emotion.

"Trust in the Lord with all your heart
And do not lean on your own understanding.
In all your ways, acknowledge Him,
And He will make your paths straight."

– Proverbs 3:5-6 (NKJV)

Use Your Emotions to Grow as a Person
i. Control your emotions to gain confidence.

There is a strong connection between confidence, emotional control, and the conquering of psychological habits. Over the years, through all of the surveys, interviews, and studies conducted on this topic, this is the most common and repeated truth from both participants and researchers alike: no matter what a person is trying to attempt, confidence is key!

Many different life factors can affect a person's self-esteem and confidence, with adolescence taking the largest toll on a person's view of themselves. However, you always have the opportunity to take action to improve your self-esteem and confidence levels and thereby improve your overall life satisfaction and path to reaching your goals.

ii. Record your emotions to become more aware of your feelings.

Keeping a journal is a great strategy to help organize your thoughts. People tend to underestimate the power of noting down their thoughts every day. Journaling enables you to rid your mind of negative emotions that you might not otherwise be aware of. It enhances your working memory and guarantees that you can more effectively manage stress.

Similarly, the habit of noting down your daily experiences in a journal helps you express the emotions that may be bottled up within you. This creates mental and emotional space for you to experience new things in life. The end result is that you can relieve yourself of anxiety and negativity and explore new experiences with a positive mindset.

iii. Don't be inhibited by what people think of you.

If you truly want to beat negative thoughts and negative self-talk, identify where it comes from. People around us often condition us into believing something bad about ourselves. Even seemingly harmless or subtle negative comments or pieces of criticism can impact our sense of self-worth. The voice of others slowly and insidiously becomes our inner voice of critical self-talk. Never let someone else's perception of you define your reality or become the foundation of your self-talk.

Are there people around you who view your life, or their own, in a predominantly negative light? Are you an unwilling victim of someone else's negativity? While it isn't uncommon for negative self-talk to originate within us, it can often be traced back to our conditioning and the beliefs, actions, and words of the people around us. Critical talk originating from another person's low confidence or self-esteem is highly challenging to deal with. Run miles away from such negative and destructive people to change your outlook on life, and begin to view it more positively and constructively.

Avoid slipping into the trap of negativity laid down by others. Stay away from chronic whiners and habitual complainers. Don't validate other people's complaints by chiming in. According to a Warsaw School of Social Psychology study, people who are always complaining experience reduced life satisfaction, more extraordinary negative emotions, stunted positive thinking, and lower moods (Karim, 2020).

Tips for Developing Mental Toughness

Mental toughness is a personality trait that enables an individual to effectively face and overcome challenges, pressure, and stressors and still perform at his or her best regardless of the situation. Developing mental toughness will help you take charge of your emotions and life.

Do not get upset quickly, and stay calm and relaxed even in a stressful environment. Pray about your troubles. Believe that you can make a difference and that your life will impact the lives of others.

Stick to your goals, and evaluate them from time to time according to the facts and God's plan for your life.

Cultivate the habit of arriving on time, exercise regularly, and maintain a healthy lifestyle. Be true to your word. You don't need other people's approval to know what you're capable of. Whatever task is assigned to you, try to deliver with flying colors.

Do not be easily influenced or intimidated. See a challenge as a chance to showcase your God-given talents. Look at every problem and obstacle as a stepping stone to inspire and motivate you to push harder towards your goals. Don't give up quickly. Instead, strive to be better—

welcome challenges as opportunities for self-development. Be willing to improve and learn something valuable from every difficulty you encounter. Move forward with God on your side. Through mental toughness, you can use your emotions to grow as a person.

Build a Solid Inner Life

Having an "inner life" is a vital component of your personality to help you face tough situations. "The inner life thus is something that seems to be much fuller than just doing what ethical reason demands; it seems to involve a whole sense of a moral space in our lives that needs to be filled… Certainly, it involves a certain appreciation of the fullness of life itself" (Springsted, 2020).

Your inner life involves your state of mind, what you think about, how you address those thoughts, and the enduring qualities of your mind. Ultimately, your inner life manifests itself in your behavior. Behavior, actions, and words are all ways of expressing what's going on in your mind. You may tend to behave certain ways in certain situations, and in this way, you're expressing what's happening in your inner life.

Related to your inner life is the concept of having inner strength. Some believe that inner strength is primarily about motivation and drive, while others believe it is mainly about spiritual discovery. If we take a more tangible approach, we can define inner strength as a set of abilities and skills that enable you to survive and thrive in your surroundings. It also entails a mindset that motivates you to strive for growth and innovation.

To develop inner strength, and thereby a healthy inner life, you must first take the time to learn more about yourself, including your aspirations, values, limitations, and personal goals. Building inner strength is, in some ways, a voyage of self-discovery and self-growth, a path to becoming a better version of yourself.

The Holy Spirit has the power to build you up and produce in you a strong inner life so that you can experience happiness and peace. Remember what the Apostle Paul said:

"But the fruit of the Spirit is love, joy, peace, longsuffering, kindness, goodness, faithfulness, gentleness, self-control."

– Galatians 5:22 (NKJV)

Try to cultivate these fruits of the Spirit in yourself, and you will develop inner strength and a blessed inner life, which will, in turn, enable you to share that happiness ad peace with others.

Be yourself

Contentment is another element that is critical for mental toughness. To develop happiness, you have to learn how to be satisfied with what you have. This doesn't mean you should abandon your ambition or the desire to achieve greater success. Instead, it means you should make the effort to be grateful for the positives that currently exist in your life. After all, the only way you can truly appreciate the fulfillment of your dreams is if you first understand and accept your life the way it is.

In addition to appreciating what you have, you should be happy with who you are. Again, this doesn't mean you should settle for your current flaws and not try to improve your character, but it does mean you need to learn to appreciate who you are and the talents God has given you. There will always be issues you want to fix within yourself and things you know you could do better, but you have to love yourself, flaws and all, in order to truly improve.

When you learn to appreciate the good parts of your personality, you can pursue self-improvement with a sense of pride, hope, and optimism about who you'll become as you begin to fulfill your true potential. This occurs when you:

- Take time daily with God.
- Take time for yourself.
- Discover your identity: you are loved, you are blessed, you are unique, you have a bright future.

Discover your calling to overcome your challenges

The world is full of adventures and excitement, and only those who are confident and mentally healthy can fully explore and enjoy them. Mentally tough people are always on the go, so they discover many exciting new experiences. They learn new skills, try different activities, eat different cuisines, travel to other countries, venture into deeper conversational waters, meet new people. Mentally tough people enjoy their lives more than those who are afraid and unwilling to leave their comfort zones.

If you want to live a healthy lifestyle and overcome the challenges that come your way, you have to train yourself to see the world in a different light. The only way to do that is to step out of your comfort zone and explore! Only then will you realize that the world is a much better and more exciting place than you ever imagined it would be.

When your views of the world become positive, your mind will be healthier and stronger as well, and you'll be better equipped to overcome the hardships you may face. Eventually, you'll be able to strive harder to achieve your goals because you know that the world is not so scary after all, that everyone has a place and a role in society and in their community, and that success, joy, and peace are not at all elusive.

Several decades ago, scientists discovered that each person has a unique heartbeat. It's based on the volume and form of your heart, the direction of your valves, and your physiology. Out of the 7 billion people on this Earth, your heartbeat is unique. You are unique in the whole universe. This is just one indication to show you that you are unique in God's eyes. He takes a particular interest in you. Just believe it! God loves you. You are precious in His eyes.

God tells us:

"See, I have inscribed you on the palms of My hands; Your walls are continually before Me."

– Isaiah 49:16 (NKJV)

Do not worry about the difficulties and stresses that arise in your life. You are in God's Hands. It's time to wake up, to build your inner life and develop your mental toughness. Remind yourself that you are blessed and God loves you.

Paul said:

"Blessed be the God and Father of our Lord Jesus Christ, who has blessed us with every spiritual blessing in the heavenly places in Christ."

– Ephesians 1:3 (NKJV)

Do not let your negative emotions enslave you. Do not lose your joy by overthinking your situation. See the big picture: You have been created by God for a unique purpose. Your dreams are bigger than whatever challenges you may face. You have a mission in life. You are unique on this Earth, and you have a bright future. When you are tempted to feel discouraged, remember these words:

"The Lord has appeared of old to me, saying: Yes, I have loved you with an everlasting love; Therefore with lovingkindness I have drawn you... There is hope in your future, says the Lord..."

– Jeremiah 31:3, 17 (NKJV)

Key Takeaways

- Emotions arise from our physiology, our situation, and our interactions with others. If we allow negative emotions to take over, they can impact our health and wellbeing.

- Emotional mastery is key to helping you become mentally tough. You need to be able to recognize and control the emotions you're feeling. Writing your emotions down via journaling can be helpful, as well as reinforcing positive self-talk and turning to God in prayer.

- Mental toughness consists of control of emotions and behavior, commitment to your goals, confidence in yourself, and facing challenges without fear or trepidation. Mentally tough people experience and enjoy life's adventures to the fullest.

- A strong inner life, involving mental peace, clarity, and connection to God, will give you the mental toughness you need to transcend your moments of difficulty and experience the fullness of life.

Time to Take Action

As we have covered in this chapter, your brain can have a hard time sorting out emotions from logical reasoning, so it can be tricky to achieve emotional mastery even when you think you know the source of your feelings. We like to think we're in control, but the truth is, our unconscious mind has a much more profound impact than we might think.

Therefore, be gentle with yourself. Emotional mastery and behavioral change won't happen overnight. Take small steps toward your goals each day on the path to mental toughness and a peaceful inner life, and don't be discouraged if you still sometimes feel overwhelmed by negative emotions and thoughts. Keep trying to replace the negativity with positivity, and stay close to God so that He can give you the help you need.

Conclusion

I hope that through reading this book and implementing the suggestions contained within, you become mentally strong, positive, and free from all fears and anxieties. Now that you have gained the knowledge contained in these pages, you know how to break your bad habits of overthinking and replace them with new, constructive ones. Don't stockpile your subconscious mind with negativity, but instead, gather positive thoughts and experiences to store in your memory and draw from in difficult times.

Let's look back at what we've learned in this book:

In Chapter One, we looked at overthinking in general and the factors that cause you to overthink. Then we addressed the various forms of overthinking and how you can rescue yourself from this trap.

In Chapter Two, we saw the consequences that overthinking has on our lives, mentally, physically, and socially. But then, we found out that all is not lost—there is still hope, even for the worst overthinker.

Chapter Three brought forward a variety of ways to eliminate overthinking, and we went further and addressed why you need a happy life that is not filled with negative thoughts. Endurance and becoming unbreakable under God's refuge crowned this chapter.

Everything starts in the mind, and that is why Chapter Four brought us to mental clarity. The brain is relatively tiny, but a lot happens there, and we addressed the importance of mental clarity in your life. Because stress kicks in when the mind is overanalyzing, achieving mental clarity is a crucial step towards eliminating overthinking.

Chapter Five addressed the concept of stress management. We examined the causes of everyday stressors in our lives and strategies for managing that stress.

Mental clutter is a key source of stress; thus, in Chapter Six, we looked at ways to declutter our minds and life. We looked at how to identify our core values and how to set up SMART goals and follow through on them.

In Chapter Seven, we discovered ways of cultivating new attitudes and addressing our anger. We go further. In particular, we discussed how DBT therapy can assist in the journey of managing anger and other negative emotions.

Finally, in Chapter Eight, we reached the peak of our journey, where we addressed living a purposeful life by mastering our emotions and finding our inner strength. We can conclude that the call to this journey starts with you.

Practice all the exercises and good habits found in these chapters to maintain your physical and mental health. After reading this book, you should:

- have the skills to control your life and desire to make positive changes;

- through God's grace, feel secure that no challenging situation can stop you;

- make the right decisions and spread love and joy to all your loved ones;

- be stable and calm, without going to extremes;

- focus on achieving your goals and create some time to pamper yourself;

- fill your heart with joy and not with the grief of sorrow and misery;

- take time to meditate on God's Word;

- take care of your mind and body and exercise daily, for this marks the beginning of a healthy life;

- cultivate your relationships, which are the number one predictor of your future wellbeing; and

- always be close to God, who is the controller of our lives.

Remember, there are two types of change: Rapid, superficial change can cause a temporary feeling of happiness, but eventually lands you right back where you started; on the other hand, continuous, incremental growth through small changes will enable you to create lasting positivity in your life. The single most important question here is: What will you do differently from now on? Take action to produce mental and behavioral change *now*. This is the core of all self-improvement.

Do not surrender to overthinking, anxiety, and fear. Develop your inner life daily. Balance your life in such a way that you can experience joy, love, hope, and peace in the emotional, physical, spiritual, and psychological dimensions. Do not overthink or shy away from challenging situations; instead, have faith that with God's grace, you will make it through.

"I can do all things through Christ who strengthens me."
Philippians 4:13 (NKJV)

Thank You

Thank you so much for purchasing my book.

You could have picked any other book, but you chose this one.

So, THANK YOU for getting this book and for making it all the way to the end.

Before you go, I wanted to ask you for one small favor. Could you please consider posting a review on Amazon? Posting a review is the best and easiest way to spread the information contained in this book.

Your feedback will help me to write the kinds of books that will help you in your spiritual growth. It would mean a lot to me to hear from you.

PLEASE LEAVE YOUR REVIEW

References

Andersson, G., Carlbring, P., Titov, N., & Lindefors, N. (2019). Internet interventions for adults with anxiety and mood disorders: A narrative umbrella review of recent meta-analyses. *The Canadian Journal of Psychiatry, 64*(7), 465–470. doi:10.1177/0706743719839381

Facts and statistics. Anxiety & Depression Association of America. (2021). Retrieved from https://adaa.org/understanding-anxiety/facts-statistics

Brown, K. W., & Ryan, R. M. (2003). The benefits of being present: Mindfulness and its role in psychological well-being. *Journal of Personality and Social Psychology, 84*(4), 822–848. doi:10.1037/0022-3514.84.4.822

De Meza, D., & Dawson, C. (2020). Neither an optimist nor a pessimist be: Mistaken expectations lower well-being. *Personality and Social Psychology Bulletin, 47*(4), 540–550. doi:10.1177/0146167220934577

Garcia, I., & O'Neil, J. (2021). Anxiety in adolescents. *The Journal for Nurse Practitioners, 17*(1), 49–53. doi:10.1016/j.nurpra.2020.08.021

Grzybowski, J. (2021). *Self-talk and mindfulness: A correlational analysis* (doctoral dissertation, Middle Tennessee State University).

Hearlson, C. L. (2021). The invention of clutter and the new spiritual discipline of decluttering. *International Journal of Practical Theology, 25*(2), 224–242. doi:10.1515/ijpt-2020-0062

Heckman, W. (2019). *42 worrying workplace stress statistics.* The American Institute of Stress. Retrieved from https://www.stress.org/42-worrying-workplace-stress-statistics

Howard, J. (2019). *Cognitive errors and diagnostic mistakes.* Springer International Publishing.

Kaida, K., & Kaida, N. (2019). The sleep belief-practice index (SBPI) for the discrepancies between beliefs and practices on "GOOD" sleep. *Sleep Medicine, 64,* S183–S184. doi:10.1016/j.sleep.2019.11.507

Kalin, N. H. (2020). The critical relationship between anxiety and depression. *American Journal of*

Psychiatry, 177(5), 365–367.
doi:10.1176/appi.ajp.2020.20030305

Karim, F. (2020). Social media use and its connection to mental health: A systematic review. *Cureus, 12*(6), e8627. doi:10.7759/cureus.8627

Low, A., & McCraty, R. (2018). Heart rate variability: New perspectives on assessment of stress and health risk at the workplace. *Heart and Mind, 2*(1), 16–27. doi:10.4103/hm.hm_11_18

Nelson-Coffey, K. (2022). *The science of happiness in positive psychology 101*. Positive Psychology. Retrieved from https://positivepsychology.com/happiness/

Reeve, J., & Lee, W. (2019). A neuroscientific perspective on basic psychological needs. *Journal of Personality, 87*(1), 102–114. doi:10.1111/jopy.12390

Shah, S. M. A., Mohammad, D., Qureshi, M. F. H., Abbas, M. Z., & Aleem, S. (2020). Prevalence, psychological responses and associated correlates of depression, anxiety and stress in a global population, during the coronavirus disease (COVID-19) pandemic. *Community Mental Health Journal, 57*(1), 101–110. doi:10.1007/s10597-020-00728-y

Springsted, E. O. (2020). Having an inner life. In S. Bourgault & J. Daigle (Eds.), *Simone Weil, beyond ideology?* (pp. 25–39). Palgrave Macmillan. doi:10.1007/978-3-030-48401-9_2

Swift, P., Cyhlarova, E., Goldie, I., & O'Sullivan, C. (2014). Living with anxiety: Understanding the role and impact of anxiety in our lives. Mental Health Foundation. Retrieved from https://www.mentalhealth.org.uk/publications/living-with-anxiety

Thomas, K., & Aiken, L. (1973). Systematic relaxation to reduce preoperative stress. *Nursing Research, 22*(1), 93. doi:10.1097/00006199-197301000-00138

Wong, M. (2014). *Stanford study finds walking improves creativity*. Stanford News. Retrieved from https://news.stanford.edu/2014/04/24/walking-vs-sitting-042414/

Made in the USA
Monee, IL
02 November 2022

17000761R00115